Caravan '88

by Ursula McCafferty

Caravan '88

by Ursula McCafferty

Cover photo - Keukenhof Gardens, Amsterdam

This book is printed on recycled paper

Printed in the United States of America

Table of Contents

Table of Photographs

FOREWORD

My husband Hugh was always an avid camper and hiker so it's not surprising that, as a young family with five children, camping was not only our choice of vacations but also a financial necessity. The habit remained our way of life long after the children left the nest.

As we got older, a motor home replaced the wall tent. We covered lots of territory from Alaska to Mexico and had dreams of, some day, traveling across Australia. Although we were both born in Europe (Hugh was born in Scotland and I in Germany), we had never planned a European camping trip. That all changed after Hugh read an article in a magazine. It was a write-up about a camping tour entitled Slo'-Poke® Caravans that sounded like a great idea, "Travel to 28 countries in the comfort of your own vehicle," "WOW"!

But then reality set in… "How much? How long? Can we do it?"

It sounded like a dream trip but we weren't sure we could manage the fees. We filed the piece for future reference and went on with our lives. But tantalizing ideas have a way of haunting you. Before long, we had written for the information, juggled our budget, said, "Why not!" and signed on. The die was cast!

This tour was designed, planned and coordinated by a retired US Army Colonel, Jim Hayden and his wife Duby. It was named Slo'-Poke Caravans® because it was designed for leisurely travel. No rush to leave your luggage in front of your hotel room at 5:30 a.m. and get ready to board a bus at 7. Except for special situations, like ferry schedules, the pace was up to the individual couple. It became one of the most memorable trips we ever took.

The preparations required obtaining new passports and a variety of visas, purchasing the necessary vehicle, a VW camper to be picked up in Germany, and lots of Travelers Checks. It was 1988 and Europe was not yet a wide-open, boundary-less continent. Part of the journey was behind the iron curtain and the Berlin Wall was still in place. Communism still reigned in many places but we were assured that we would have safe passage.

Travel with me as I relive the journey of a lifetime.

Chapter 1 ~ SLO'POKE®

After we mailed our deposit for the Slo'-Poke Caravans®, the information began flooding in. Twenty-five couples were signed up. We would be touring for five months in our campers. The travelers would gather, on April 19, in Illinois and fly from Chicago's O'Hare airport. Our luggage was to consist of one duffle bag each with our name stenciled on the side, and one box containing a "Porto-Potty."

Our rendezvous point was at a Holiday Inn in Des Plaines, Illinois. We left our home in Florida the morning of April 18. I did all the driving because Hugh didn't like driving my car and we didn't want to make the trip in his little pick-up. We took our time and spent the night in a Holiday Inn. After a hearty breakfast we did the last leg of the tip to Des Plaines arriving at the rendezvous in mid-afternoon. Our first meeting was scheduled for early evening. After we checked into our hotel room we went to the hotel restaurant for a late lunch. A couple was seated at the next table and on a hunch I asked them if they were with Slo'-Poke Caravans®. It was a good guess; they were from Canada and were to become close friends in the months ahead and for years beyond. Storage for our car had been pre-arranged in a long, long shed at a mushroom farm outside of town. It would languish there until October.

Our first briefing gave us the opportunity to meet our leaders and our other fellow travelers. The group consisted of people from all parts of the USA, and one couple from Canada, almost all retired couples except two teachers on sabbatical leave. Few still working people could hardly take off from work for six long months.

We were impressed with Jim and Duby Hayden's know how. They had traveled extensively in Europe while stationed in Germany post WWII. They used their knowledge and experience to map the entire journey from highways, miles of travel per day, campgrounds, points of special interest to special tours. The whole group was an interesting mix and we looked forward to making some solid friendships.

After a hardy breakfast and a group photo op we were bussed to busy O'Hare airport. While waiting to check in we were all grouped around our luggage. Our duffle bags stood out among the rest because we had bought bright red ones, easy to spot in a luggage check line. The Porto-Potty, with its' picture on the outside of the box, left nothing to the imagination and drew more than one snicker from observers. We actually must have made quite a picture, 40+ people, many gray-haired, wearing blue and white Slo'-Poke® caps, hauling around duffel bags and Porto-Pottys! Fortunately, the luggage was ticketed through to our trans-Atlantic flight so we only had to deal with the Porto-Potty boxes at O'Hare.

Photo #1 ~ The whole Slo'-Poke® Gang

When we received our tickets we discovered that we would be flying from O'Hare to JFK in New York, and from NY to Holland. If we had asked the right questions we would have known in advance that we would make our ultimate departure from JFK. We could have driven to New York in half the time, visited our family and met the group in New York. Of course, we would then have missed the briefing and the opportunity to meet all our fellow travelers on day one.

The flight to Amsterdam went without a hitch. I guess I was too keyed up to sleep, but I did get in a few winks before raising the shade and watching the sunrise. With the six-hour difference between New York and Europe you are flying into the breaking dawn in the middle of your night. The trick is to not sleep until bedtime in Europe. That puts your system on Euro time a lot easier.

As we approached Schiphol air terminal in Amsterdam it looked huge. Once we entered the terminal it seemed even larger. The facility was very impressive and customs clearance was smooth and efficient. Our group quickly gathered to board a chartered bus for our trip to Wiedenbrück and the Westfalia plant where our VW vans had been converted into campers.

When we crossed the border into Germany I had this uncanny feeling of coming home. I had left Germany as a five year old and had never been back, and yet, I had that strange feeling.

At a rest stop on the Autobahn we had our first experience with European rest rooms. There is no set fee for the use of the restrooms but there is always a matron in attendance and with the matron there is always a dish for contributions. This was no exception to the rule. Having just landed, none of us had a single Deutsche Mark to our name and what US cash we had was tucked away in our luggage. Fortunately I speak German well enough to apologize and explain to the matron why we couldn't contribute. She was far more gracious than many other "rest room dragons" I encountered over the next several months.

When the bus rolled into Wiedenbrück we were delighted with the atmosphere, the old world architecture and the warm welcome we received from the Volkswagen representative. We were wined, dined and quartered in the local hotel. It was a lovely evening, but it had been a long 24hours and the arms of Morpheus were beckoning. We spent, what was to be our last night in months, in real beds.

The following morning (4/21) we headed to the Westfalia plant and were introduced to our new homes, a line-up of white campers sporting a blue stripe and with a number on each. Hugh and I were given the keys to #107.

We had a briefing on the how's and wherefores' of raising the top to create an upper bunk bed, how to refill the propane tank that fuels the stove and refrigerator. We found all the storage areas, made lists of what we would need for creature comforts and loaded on our duffel bags. The precious Porto-Potty was concealed in a specially designed box topped with a cushion. (an extra seat for guests! If only they knew!)

The staff at Westfalia gave us a great lunch and a hearty send-off. At 2:30 p.m. our journey began. We all had our Travel Log with complete directions but for this first jaunt we convoyed to the Marktkauf (super market) to get our supplies. We bought pots and pans, dishes, clothes hangers, pillows, folding chairs and groceries and even an emergency breakdown kit. I wasn't as good in German as I thought; I couldn't remember what the correct name was for a kleiderbügel (clothes hangar). Fortunately we had a guide with us to do any necessary translating. We finally hit the road again at 6:00 p.m. headed for our first campground.

We reached Touma campground in Tecklenburg at 7:30 and our new odometer read 49 miles! Fortunately there was a good restaurant on the premises so we had "dinner out".

We set up the upper bunk but I found it extremely awkward to climb up and down. I was also afraid of taking a nasty fall so we regrouped; all our "stuff" from the back deck went up into the upper bunk and we set up the lower bed. This involved dropping the back of the rear bench to level with the back deck making reasonable bed. It wasn't quite a double bed but a good three-quarter. We had plenty of room because we were not large people but a 200-pound six-footer would have had a little problem. My only problem was that I was miserable! I had become accustomed to a waterbed at home and this bed was so hard that I couldn't get comfortable. It was evident that we would have to make some kind of adjustment. But the night passed and I greeted the new day at 5:30 a.m. by going to the big, clean bathroom and taking a nice hot shower. The facilities in Touma campground were excellent, something we would wistfully look back on later in our journey.

The International Camping Caravan group hosted us during our stay at Touma Campground April 22nd & 23rd. The days were filled with planned activities. At noon it was "up to the restaurant for a pigs hocks dinner" (really tasty). At 3:00 p.m. it was coffee and fresh "Berliner" (a raised doughnut sprinkled with sugar). At 6:00p.m., supper was served from huge caldrons of homemade mushroom soup that beat any canned version you could think of. But there was more; we went back to the restaurant for a beer and wine gathering followed by a magic show. The hospitality was amazing. Finally we wandered back to our #107 and crawled into bed. It was cold out but April in North Germany is still a cold time of year. When you look at the world map and see that New York City and Rome are approximately at the same latitude it puts things into perspective.

I don't know if I was just very tired or was adjusting to the hard bed, but I slept better.

The next morning, after a leisurely breakfast cooked in our own rig, we joined a walking tour of Tecklenburg, another picturesque town. The weather was clear and the air crisp, a good day for a walk. We stopped in a café for a coffee break and then headed back to camp. When we arrived lunch was waiting for us—caldrons of homemade pea soup.

This was our last day with our German friends and they outdid themselves. In England it's afternoon tea and crumpets but in Germany it's afternoon coffee and "torte mit schlag" (torte with whipped cream). How could we refuse? At 7:30 we were wined and dined again, this time with Bratwurst, music, dancing and lots of good conversation and camaraderie.

We were scheduled to leave for Holland in the morning. As a special treat, one of the German couples, the Schoegels, invited us to breakfast in their trailer. They were from Hamburg, my hometown, and we had developed quite a friendship with them that continued over many more years.

At 9:30 a.m. on April 24th the long awaited journey began in earnest.

Chapter 2 ~ Holland, Belgium & Luxembourg

April 24th:

The 162-mile drive to Camping Het Amsterdam was leisurely and picturesque. This amazing country built, in many places at the very edge of the sea, was devoid of hills, cliffs or mesas but it was immaculate. There was no litter along the highway, no trash bags on the shoulder of the road; quite a change from some of our own roads.

All the campers rolled in on time and no one got lost. It was our first night on the actual journey and we cooked supper in our own little "kitchen." Things got a little mixed up but we established a system and our first dinner was a success. We tidied up, took a walk around the park and headed for an early bed. Our odometer read 230mi.

April 25th:

We got an early start on our first group bus tour. It began at Maarken and was followed by a ferry trip to Volendam for lunch. We tried the local specialties and I discovered that smoked eel is really delicious. From Volendam it was back on the bus to Edam. Of course we bought a whole cheese. Our final stop was Zaanse Schans to visit the working windmills. In one of the windmills they make wonderful mustard and sell it in lovely Delft jars. We bought a little jar and I treasured it long after the mustard was gone.

We only got lost twice on the way back to camp but we were not alone!

April 26th:

This was a free day and we spent the time exploring the area on our own.

Photo #2 ~ Windmills in Holland

In Amstelven we found a hardware store, a department store and a wonderful food market. Instead of going to the flower auction the following day we chose to spend the time shopping. Our most important purchase was a pair of air mattresses! Ahhhh! We cashed travelers checks, bought a dishpan, coffee pot and some delicious deli food. We were amazed at the perfect English being spoken by one of the deli clerks. We told her that we were impressed at her perfect English and she quickly solved the mystery with the following answer, "I _AM_ English!"

The only thing we didn't get done was laundry. We wound up doing it by hand, outside, in cement tubs, in cold water! Our hands were numb when we finished. We learned quickly that, in Europe, every village and town does not have a Laundromat.

Our sightseeing and shopping tours added 93 miles to our Odometer: 323mi.

April 27th:

We had heard of the Keukenhof Gardens and the tulip display and were delighted to spend the following day (April 28th) strolling through acres of formal gardens. The gardens were magnificent and we spent hours taking pictures of colorful beds of tulips, fragrant hyacinths, and lily ponds.

We had the opportunity to buy bulbs and have them shipped home but it would be many months before we would be home again so we showed restraint.

After all that walking we were pleased that our caravan was allowed to spend the night in the Keukenhof parking area.

Miles today: 20 Odom: 343

April 29th:

Today we went to Madurodam, an amazing miniature village showing all elements of life in Holland; it's located in the city of Schevenigen and covers a small city block. One could spend hours just watching all the miniature activity but we didn't stay long; we had an errand to fulfill.

We joined the Haydens, Stones and Kents, on a day-long journey, to pick up the awnings for all the campers. The trip took us straight through Belgium, down to the French border. After picking up all the awnings, and radios we headed to Antwerp and from Antwerp to Bemelen, our next camp. It was a very long day. We, and the rest of the "awning crew," went out for supper. That, in itself, was an adventure. We finally called it a night at 10:10 p.m.

Miles today: 321 Odom: 664mi.

April 30th-May 1st:

Two quiet days were spent in camp. Hugh was feeling a little under the weather so the break was a good thing. Everyone was busy installing awnings, radios and rear window guards. The window guard did double duty. Not only did the guard protect our rear window from kicked up gravel or stones, it made a handy drying rack for small laundry items when we were stationary.

We did some more exploring. We refilled our propane tank and took a ride to Aachen looking for, of all things, ice cream! But it was Sunday and everything was closed so we meandered back to camp. We went to the camp restaurant for supper and were entertained by a delightful band concert.

Miles today: 60 Odom: 724 mi.

May 2nd:

This was the beginning of a nostalgic and somewhat sad part of our journey. We visited the first of the cemeteries of our war dead in Margraten.

To see the crosses lined up row on row brought a lump to our throats...all those brave men that never came home.

We needed an emotional boost so, with several of our fellow travelers, we set off for the city of Tongeren, the oldest city in Belgium. We shopped for groceries and gas using our Belgian currency, which was a little confusing.

So many years before the Euro we were obliged to use different currencies each time we crossed into another country.

From Tongeren it was on to Liege, but we got a little lost. By some miracle we found the Autobahn and signs for Bastogne, our next rendezvous. We arrived safely in Bastogne at 2:00p.m. From there it was a short run to Parc Exposition, our next overnight spot. We joined the Peters and visited the "Nuts" museum, then on to the spot where General Patton broke through the German lines in WWII.

The "Nuts" museum commemorates an incident during the "Battle of the Bulge" and General Anthony McAuliffe's reply to the German demand for surrender.

Historically it was a very interesting day but emotionally it was draining.

9

We looked forward to a side trip to Luxembourg the next day.

Miles today: 98 Odom: 822.

The beauty of this tour was the ability to explore on your own. It was just necessary, for security reasons, to notify our leader if we intended to be off tour overnight or even for a few days. Hugh and I departed the tour temporarily several times to visit our own birthplaces, living relatives and points of special interest to us. We always made clear when and where we would rejoin the group. This day we explored Luxembourg beginning at Wiltz. The countryside is beautiful, a real fairy tale land. We had a great lunch in the cafeteria of a hotel in Esch. We just fell in love with the place; could have spent a month in the country. There were campgrounds everywhere. On the other hand, the city of Luxembourg was a zoo. We never stopped to see the sites because it was pouring and traffic was stop and go. We headed out of town and back to our campsite in Bastogne by way of Martelange. After a successful hunt for gasoline we arrived at camp at 5:45 p.m. in showery weather.

Miles today: 141, Odom: 963.

Chapter 3 ~ France

May 4th:

Wednesday dawned gloomy and gray with showers. At 8:30 a.m. we gathered for a trip to Bouillon Castle. The castle was an interesting ruin and we enjoyed it in spite of the showery weather. The feudal castles were always built on a high point overlooking a valley or a river. It gave the occupants the benefit of an unobstructed view of possible approaching enemies. I couldn't help pitying the poor serfs that had to carry all the building supplies up the steep mountainsides.

In clearing weather, we drove on to Reims to see the cathedral. The cathedral is a classic beauty; it was a privilege to explore it. Our stay in Reims was just long enough to visit the cathedral, grab some lunch and head for Épernay. The trip down was relaxing and pleasant and then…we all got lost looking for the camp. Due to construction, the road had been changed since the log was written. But our leader managed to round us up from all the corners of town and we arrived safely. Our next big chore, as usual, was for the next day when we would have to get our laundry done, by hand, in cold water. But first on the agenda was a tour of the Champagne cellars.

Today's miles: 137 Odom: 1100

May 5th:

The tour was an eye opener; I never realized that there was so much involved. We were never big champagne drinkers but after the whole process was explained and we had the grand tour of the cool cellars we could understand what makes it a favorite "special" for celebrations and occasions.

Our tour leader told us a story of an earlier champagne tour. Evidently one of the tour members was known to be very thrifty and a real bargain hunter. While many of the group bought champagne at the on site shop this man went shopping elsewhere. At the customary evening happy hour he boasted of the great bargain he found in a super market…a whole case of champagne for a fraction of the price the others had paid on the tour. He proudly shared a bottle. Unfortunately it was undrinkable. The only thing on the label he understood was the word champagne but not the word vinaigre. No one ever found out what he did with the remaining bottles. Another example of "If it's too good to be true, it probably isn't."

Hugh and I had made a habit of having fresh bread, fruit and cheese for our breakfast. We had started out in Holland with a whole Edam cheese and we stocked up different cheese whenever we had the opportunity. To find fresh bread we had to develop a technique. In the morning, we parked on the main street in almost any town in France and waited. We could guarantee that, before long, someone would walk, or ride a bicycle, passed our van and return in a few minutes with a loaf of bread under their arm (hence our habit of referring to the long baguettes as "armpit" bread). The trick was to observe the person on their first pass and watch where they went. Invariably they would disappear into some ordinary building, with no signs above the door, and emerge with fresh bread. All we had to do was grab a handful of francs, head for the same door, smile, point at the loaves and hold out a hand with the money. The baker would take what he needed for the loaf, wrap it in paper, smile and thank us, and we would be off with our fresh loaf. A few of our fellow travelers always marveled at the fact that we had found a place to buy fresh bread. We also managed to find every pastry shop in France (and later in Germany and Austria). I'm sure that is what caused our less than streamlined figures when we finally got home. For the rest of our shopping we found a Co-Op store and bought fish for dinner and some luscious pates for the following days lunch.

Tomorrow, Paris!

Mileage to and from Coop: 2 Odom: 1102

May 6th:

We visited Château-Thierry and Belleau Wood, World War I Battlefields. No matter which war, the sorrow is always there for the many that died on the battlefields. Although these are great historical sites I found them very depressing. I looked forward to the hustle and bustle of our next stop, Paris, the city of light.

The trip was clearly outlined and we had only a minor problem when we thought we had missed a turn and backtracked. While backtracking three of our group passed us at an intersection. When we were getting turned around again a motorcycle policeman appeared, hailed us to follow him (and a paddy wagon) and led us right into the camp. Evidently the paddy wagon was not for us because it continued on past our turnoff.

It was 2:30 p.m. and we hoped to find a bank to cash travelers checks and acquire francs. I went with another couple, the Harts, and what should have been a simple procedure turned into something else. At the first bank we entered they just shook their heads when we presented travelers checks. Since we didn't speak French and they obviously didn't speak English we just left and looked for another bank. The second bank also gave us a cold shoulder.

There were two people sitting at a desk, one a stern looking woman who just shook her head and the other, a young man. It took me a minute to realize that the young man was dropping hints with an English word scattered among the rapid French. He kept glancing at the stern woman almost to see if she was catching on to the fact that he was actually trying to be helpful. His message was, "Go across the street." The "street" was a five-lane highway with cars going in all directions. I had seen movies supposedly filmed in Paris and had always assumed that the mad traffic scenes were staged for effect. To face the reality was something of a shock. By some miracle we made it across and located yet another bank. They took our travelers checks, almost threw our money at us, no "Have a good day", no "Goodbye. " We had just experienced a side of Paris that none of us forgot… " If you don't speak French you're chopped liver!" We actually crossed that highway once more and succeeded in getting back to camp alive. Tomorrow we will have a bus tour of the city.

Miles today: 106 Odom: 1208

May 7th:

We boarded our bus at 9a.m. for an extensive tour. We saw the Louvre, the opera house, Montmartre, Moulin Rouge, Sacré-Cœur and the river Seine. We stopped at the Eiffel tower for photo-ops and at Notre Dame cathedral. We did enter Notre Dame but it was an incredible mob scene of tourists and tour guides and vendors. We didn't linger. Hugh commented that Christ had thrown the money-lenders out of the temple and the chaos in Notre Dame was as bad.

Photo #3 ~Moulin Rouge

We got back to camp late morning and decided to go shopping. Betty and Larry Peters and Duby Hayden joined us and we got lost. With the help of some friendly gendarmes we got turned around the right way and back to camp. The camp was well patrolled by police. It was very comforting because, by its' location, the camp was accessible to any pedestrians who might chose to meander through and, maybe, pick up a few carelessly left out items at the individual campsites.

The campground had a little restaurant, bar and grocery store that was managed by a young Vietnamese man. For no reason we could think of, he immediately adopted us and insisted on referring to Hugh and me as "My Fadduh and Muddah." He was quite excited to speak to people from the state of Connecticut because his brother lived nearby (in Boston). It reminded me of another story: A man asked an American tourist if he possibly knew his brother in America. When asked where his brother lived he replied, "Oh just around the corner in Chicago."

May 8th & 9th:

(Mother's Day) We were free both days to explore, shop or just loaf. We shopped at the supermarket and visited our camp store and our Vietnamese friend and relaxed. Some of our group took public transportation and visited various landmarks and points of interest but we were just happy to loaf.

It rained on Monday, so the scheduled tour through the sewers of Paris was cancelled. I can honestly say that I was not sorry. Somehow the idea of wandering around in the sewers of Paris didn't really thrill me.

We called two of our clan just to touch base and let them know where their parents were. Our TV at home always came on at 10 p.m. with the message, "Do you know where your children are?" We always imagined that our children were saying, "Do we know where our parents are?"

May 10th:

We got an early start for Versailles. The traffic was terrible, the chateau was mobbed and I felt rotten. I had the sniffles and a pounding headache. Rather than join the group on the tour of the chateau, I curled up on the bunk to sleep. I had just dozed off when Hugh and Jim (our leader) came back. Our friend Larry had collapsed. Jim grabbed the emergency oxygen tank from his van and we piled into Larry's vehicle to head up to the chateau. I made up the bed in the back of the van so that we could transport Larry to the hospital if necessary. Hugh was designated driver; he turned left at a no left turn sign and crossed three lanes of traffic to get from the parking area up to the door of the chateau. It was the sort of wild ride akin to "Mr. Frog's Wild Ride" at Disney World. How I ever got that bed put together without landing on the floor in a heap was nothing short of a miracle. Fortunately Larry survived and we all got safely to our next camp, Camping Parc Omni Sports.

The camp was great, hot water for dishes and good hot showers. We took a short walk from the camp to a nice food shop and bought some delicious veal "rolladen" and French pastry for dessert, yum! The rolladen consist of a thin filet of veal (or beef) rolled up and skewered, with a slice of bacon, pickle and onion inside.

The following day I slept most of the day and began to feel much better. (Have to credit the pastry!)

Miles today: 31 Odom: 1239

May 12th:

Hated to leave our very nice camp but it was onward ever onward; next stops Chartres and Châteaudun.

Quite a few of the group rolled out in a bunch but we took our time leaving and went on our own. Before long we caught up to and passed the few that were dawdling at 30 mph. We had no trouble locating the Cathedral in Chartres and after a quiet visit we headed on to Châteaudun. We found a supermarket as we entered the town, shopped for the scheduled potluck supper for that evening, filled the gas tank and found the camp with no problems.

The camp manager was a woman who lived on the premises. When she was not conducting camp business she wore her apron. When she was "official" she wore an official, peaked cap. She was a delightful little woman and the most mouth-watering aromas from her kitchen made everyone hungry.

The camp description mentioned fresh bread delivery to the camp so Hugh, in his best high school French, asked Madame when the bakery truck would come. She kept shaking her head and pointing in the general direction of the village and saying "A pied" and slapping her knee! Very strange...until Hugh figured out that she was telling him "on foot into town." In other words, take a hike, walk to the bakery, there is no delivery! We walked and found the bakery but it wasn't open. So much for "a pied."

We were becoming a more cohesive group, getting to know each other better.

Our potluck supper that night was a great success. My contribution was a batch of 30 meatballs that disappeared in a flash. There was lots of good food, delicious desserts and the wine flowed like water.

Châteaudun campground was also our initiation to French bathroom facilities.

I planned a nice hot shower before bed but, when I walked into the building where the bath facilities were located, the first thing I saw was a man standing at a urinal relieving himself. I did a quick U turn and headed back to our home-away-from-home and took a sponge bath. I got a little tougher as time went on. Miles today, include a return trip to the store and a search for propane.

Miles today: 87 miles Odom: 1326

May 13th:

Today we started our second longest day trip to date at 8. Jim and Duby Hayden were in the lead, the Arnolds were in the "rocking chair" position and Hugh and I were the "back door." The Arnolds had run into a few problems so, for this day, we convoyed.

We drove through the lovely Loire Valley taking time to photograph some beautiful scenery. We stopped at huge château Chambord for photos and continued on to a smaller, beautiful château eau Chenonceau that was built in 1551 on the site of an earlier manor. Chenonceau was built for the Emperor's mistress. It was luxurious. With all the excessiveness of the royalty it's a small wonder the peasants didn't rebel sooner.

17

Photo #4 ~ Chambord

It was a delightful, relaxing day but with miles to go we headed for our next camp at Angoulême. It began to rain and we rolled into camp at 7:30 p.m.

Miles today: 248.5 Odom: 1578

May 14th:

After a quiet, restful night, we left the camp at Angoulême at 8:30 for the easy run to Bordeaux. En route we took a side trip to Saint-Émilion, an interesting old walled city. We found a pastry shop (we had become pretty good at that) bought croissants and things like large jelly doughnuts. These were devoured at the first roadside rest area and were called "breakfast." We also found a butcher/deli and bought food for lunch. Hugh chose a little pizza and I opted for a small quiche. Two small cheese tarts rounded out the lunch menu. (Please note the well-balanced and nutritious diet.) It was after the rest area at St. Vincent de Paul that we got messed up. We took the

"Auto" route, got off, got on, and got lost. We finally got it all sorted out and rolled into camp at 2:30 p.m.

Miles today: 121 Odom: 1699

May 15th:

We took a day trip with Duby and Jim to the village of Arcachon, right on the coast. We explored the village and then opted for a seafood dinner that consisted of broiled shellfish. It was very tasty, but for some reason, it did not sit well with me. As we headed back to camp the sky clouded over and we ran into some heavy rain. Before turning in for the night we called our three sons to touch base.

May 16th:

At 6:00 we awoke to rain. We left camp at 8.00 a.m. and traveled with Peters and Kents today. Our target for days end was Bayonne but we had the time to explore. We took a secondary road to a beach town with a lighthouse, Contais-les-Bains. We thought we were the only ones of our group to find the place but when we reached the beach another couple from our tour was strolling barefoot along the beach. And we had thought we were so clever.

We got a little confused when we were entering Bayonne but found the camp with no problem. The sky had cleared when we arrived, but clouded over again. Each day we look forward to what tomorrow will bring.

Miles today: 158 Odom: 1857

May 17th:

Another lazy morning start. We loafed this morning; didn't leave camp until 10:20 and then got lost leaving Bayonne. We were so intent on not missing our turn that we turned too soon. Once we realized our mistake we back-tracked and did it right. We made a direct run to St. Jean-Pied-de-Port in the Pyrenees Basque country.

19

We loved it. The town was small enough for us to walk everywhere. We strolled to the top of the citadel and enjoyed a grand view of the town below.

We had lunch and dinner at an outdoor café that served the most delicious crepes. Here, away from the big cities, the people were far friendlier and far more likeable. We managed very well with our sign language, dictionary and a smile. Just before we called it a night, a shepherd wandered through the camping area herding his sheep homeward. It was a tranquil way to end the day.

Tomorrow–Spain, a new country, a new experience. Life is good.

Mileage today: 44 Odom: 1901

Chapter 4 ~ Spain

May 18th:

Our road took us through the beautiful Pyrenees Mountains today. The border crossing was just a wave of the hand pass, no passports or visas checked. We passed a 12th century monastery nestled in the mountains at Roncesvalles and then stopped to shop in the village of Olite. We bought fresh oranges and wonderful cookies at an open-air market and fresh bread at a small grocery store. With the warmer weather we were finding flies to be a real nuisance and were anxious to find a fly swatter. In our finest pantomime we described our needs to the shopkeeper. She promptly produced a fly swatter and even told us what to call it, (phonetically pronounced...Moosh tapeta!) I have checked my Spanish dictionary to no avail ...tapeta means small carpet but where the "moosh" came from I do not know. However I will never look at a fly swatter again without thinking of the little store Olite, Spain. It's fun to see the expression on the faces of the great-grandkids when you ask them to get the "moosh tapeta!"

We happily meandered on, munching on the cookies and oranges, into Pamplona. The bulls weren't running, thanks goodness, but we managed to get lost. Do you see a pattern here? Finally, back on track, we reached Tudela and, yes we got lost again. I think that getting lost added a little excitement to the journey. We always saw a few things not included in the log and always found our way to camp. This time the camp was in Soria with a nice restaurant on the premises. It was also our first experience with Gypsies; they were all over the place. The park had a very pretty fountain that the Gypsy women were using to wash their clothing. When I was in the ladies room and combing my hair in front of the mirror, two of the Gypsy women wanted to "borrow" lipstick from me. I could honestly tell them that I didn't have any in my pocket.

At 7:30 we still were missing three couples. At 8 two arrived but the third couple was still missing. Our group considered backtracking to see if they had perhaps broken down. Before we could put that plan into action, the missing couple went rolling by on the highway. Fortunately they spotted us madly waving and calling out to them. They found a place to turn around and head back to the camp. For everyone's safety it was important that everyone be accounted for at the end of each day. The missing couple had previous problems and all were concerned for their safety so we gave a sigh of relief when they arrived.

Miles today: 171 Odom: 2072

May 19th:

It was a grand day. The scenery was very reminiscent of Wyoming, and in places, the North Dakota badlands. We visited the village of Medinaceli to see the remains of a great Roman arch dating back to 200 years BC. The Arch is built high on a hill and the view of the valley below is magnificent.

Photo #5 ~ Arch of Medinaceli

Today we again traveled with the Peters and Kents. It was a pleasant day and we found our campground with no problems although we overshot the entrance and had to turn back. Tomorrow we won't be driving; we're going on an all day bus tour.

Miles today: 142 Odom: 2214

May 20th:

Our bus tour took us into the heart of beautiful Madrid. We visited a large cathedral and stopped at 1:30 for a luncheon. We then visited "The Valley of the Fallen." The monument is a memorial and burial site of General Franco and 50,000 of his fallen troops. The cross on top of the monument is the largest in the world. Inside the monument walls and ceilings are covered with magnificent art, reminiscent of the Sistine Chapel in the Vatican, all very beautiful. The entire visit was a great experience, but bus tours can become tiring. Our guide, although extremely knowledgeable, talked non-stop. I wondered if he could ever run out of breath.

We returned to camp in time to join another couple on a run to the supermarket The Pryko supermarket was well stocked and close by. We planned to return to it before traveling on.

May 21st:

We slept in today, sheer luxury. Nice hot showers followed by a leisurely breakfast, who could ask for more? I gave Hugh a haircut and we went back to the Pryko supermarket with the Peters to restock some staples and fill the gas tank. Our following few nights will be dry camps (no facilities.) The rest of the day was given up to loafing and an early to bed.

Miles for shopping: 16 Odom: 2230

May 22nd:

Sunday, it was a good day to get around Madrid with traffic at the minimum. The entire run to next overnight, Cáceres, was a snap.

En route we spied several castles, proof that castles in Spain are not a myth.

We arrived in Cáceres in early afternoon. Our camping facility was in a large unpaved parking area next to show grounds. Preparations were being made for a horse show scheduled for the following day. We saw some beautiful horses being unloaded from their trailers. Unfortunately we would not be there for the show. We did get to meet lots of local people.

We had lined our vehicles up in a row and everyone popped up the roof.

Among the locals that came to stare, smile and try to communicate, were several young people, teens or a little older. They were interested in having a conversation and asked us many questions. As usual, Charades became the communication of choice; actions and gestures can speak volumes. When we were asked our next destination we told them Portugal. The comments they made implied that it was a poor choice, or that it was a poor country. Obviously they felt that their country was better. Then one young man made a comment we didn't understand, something about "tremelo." When he realized that we didn't get it, good old Charades came into play. He scooped up a handful of the gravel, cupped his hand and shook it. We got it!... EARTHQUAKE!!! He was telling us that earthquakes were common in Portugal.

From way back somewhere in my childhood I vaguely remember storks on a roof. At last, I saw the stork nests on rooftops and chimney tops. It's not a sight one sees in the USA. So much is different about Europe. There is so much more history than we have in our own young nation. Just seeing a Roman arch built before the birth of Christ was, to me, a miracle.

Miles today: 205 Odom: 2435

Chapter 5 ~ Portugal

May 23rd:

After an early start we headed for the Portuguese border. We stopped for gas and the Peters caught up with us in Valencia so we traveled together.

The border crossing was slow but simple enough. The countryside was beautiful, but the road was narrow and challenging. We passed lots of gnarled olive trees along both sides of the road and, occasionally, passed an ox cart. Everything was very "old world." Cork oak trees, the source of wine corks, are also grown in this area and the barks are harvested every 8 years. Picture that the next time you uncork a bottle of wine.

Our destination was a village called Marvão (pronounced Marvoh). Our first glimpse of it was unbelievable! It was nestled on the top of a mountain; a collection of white buildings with red tile roofs.

Photo #6 ~ Marvão on High

Up and up we went, finally entering the village through an arch barely wide enough for the campers to pass. The white houses were huddled side by side along the cobbled streets. The wall that encircled the town had gun ports and ancient cannons in place. We were assigned parking on the streets throughout the village. Our own spot was backed right up to the outer wall. The view was spectacular, the people were friendly and we fell in love with Marvão. We were treated to a wonderful luncheon, a "kitty treat" from the tour slush fund.

Gained an hour today when we crossed the Portuguese border.

Miles today: 77 Odom: 2512

We spent two wonderful days in the village and enjoyed every minute. Although none of us spoke Portuguese we managed to go shopping in the little general store. One of our friends was looking for, of all things, Johnson's baby powder, which was her talcum powder of choice. She was sure that she would never find it in this part of the world. Hugh always took the attitude that anything was worth a try. He tapped the store manager on the shoulder, and when he had his attention, he went through the motion of rocking a baby in his arms. This he quickly followed with a gesture like shaking a saltshaker. The store manager nodded enthusiastically and headed towards the rear of the shop. He returned in seconds with a familiar looking white container labeled Johnson's Baby Powder. Will wonders never cease?

Photo #7 ~ View from Marvào

Photo #8 ~ Village of Marvào

May 24th:

We left beautiful Marvão under a cloudless sky en route to Nazaré. Our road took us through many small villages, olive groves and a few larger towns. Quite a few of the group stopped in Tomar to sight see and shop.

Others went on to Fatima. I would have liked to stop at Fatima but the parking lot was jammed with tour buses and I had a stomach bug and a slight temperature so we just kept moving. I was delighted to see windmills again. They were quite different from the ones in Holland.

Photo #9 ~ Portuguese Windmill

We arrived at camp first, something we rarely did. I wondered why I was so very tired until it dawned on me that I had never reset the alarm clock when we entered Portugal. I had started my day at five a.m. instead of six; obviously a nap was in order. After some welcome sleep I felt better and we had a very nice dinner in the camp restaurant.

Miles today: 167 Odom: 2679

May 25th:

We took care of our laundry early and then took off, with the Peters, to the Nazaré beach. We parked our vans and strolled along the beach to look at several brightly painted fishing boats that were drawn up on the sand.

Hugh noticed that a man, sitting on a log down near the waters edge, was showing unusual interest in our vans. We made the decision to move the vans at intervals so that they were always in our sight. When we moved them a second time the man on the beach left. Perhaps we were being overly cautious but we had been warned to not leave our vehicles out of our sight when not in camp. After the leisurely stroll on the beach and into the souvenir shops we headed back to camp in time for dinner. The food in the camp restaurant was excellent and prices in Portugal were the cheapest we had seen so far on our journey.

Miles today: 10 Odom: 2689

May 26th:

Today Hugh and I took off on our own and went exploring. We drove down to Peniche and Cabo Carvoeiro. The Portuguese coast is beautiful. For lunch we parked on a bluff overlooking the water. It was such a beautiful spot that I took photos. After our return home, I took out those photos and painted one of the scenes on to canvas in oils. The picture still graces my wall.

We covered 98 miles just roaming and then headed back to camp. On the agenda for the evening was a potluck supper. The planned entertainment was a rousing game of charades. We were all getting pretty good at it in our every day experiences.
Tomorrow we're headed for Lisbon.

Miles today: 98 Odom: 2787

May 27th:

The drive to Lisbon was an easy run from Nazaré. In France we were always looking for bakeries for fresh bread. In Portugal we learned to spot the little bakery trucks that were making deliveries. We spotted one parked in front of a restaurant and were able to buy a loaf of bread and fresh rolls for our lunch.

We crossed the toll bridge into the city and rolled into camp without problems. Once our spot was established we headed out to the Mercado (a hyper-super market) and replenished our staples. When we returned to camp we met a young couple, not one of our tour, whose vehicle had been burglarized while parked on a street in Lisbon. Everything was gone, cash, passports and travelers checks. They were frantically trying to contact family in the USA. There was little we could do to help them but the police had been notified and an investigation was under way. This re-enforced what we had been taught, "Never leave your valuables in the vehicle, wear them in security pouches or belts on your body".

We spent the rest of the day repacking the van. Cold weather clothes were packed away and short-sleeved shirts were unpacked. We also re-organized the kitchen area and did some general house cleaning which was long overdue. Tomorrow some sightseeing is on the agenda.

Miles today: 60 Odom: 2847

May 28th:

We got an early start on our travels today and we car-pooled wherever possible. Hugh and I rode with Peters, as did the Kents. It was a little crowded but saved a few miles on our vehicle. We drove to Cabo da Roca, the most westerly point on the European continent. We stopped at a lovely restaurant and had a delicious dinner. It was pretty pricey; some of the main dishes ran 6000 escudos. The restaurant was in the street level of a building that was built on the side of a cliff. On the level below was a gorgeous swimming pool and all the men walked over to look at it. Small wonder, there was a topless beauty sunbathing at poolside.

On our return to camp we rested a little and then changed for our evening adventure. The bus tour of Lisbon by night was beautiful! We ended the day with a dinner at a Fado and Folklorico. The music was nice and the food was good but the sales pitch to sell the performers cassettes got a little too pushy. By the time our bus got us back to camp it was after midnight. It had truly been a memorable day.

May 29th:

Sunday morning—and we always had a little prayer service but this morning I cheated. I just couldn't get going in time for an 8:30 service. To top it off, we ran out of propane so we couldn't even make fresh coffee. We went to the Continente Hipermercado and bought a small camping "Gaz" stove, had lunch at the cafeteria and picked up the makings for a light supper. We bought a calling card to call our daughters—500 escudos for 50 seconds. We couldn't talk long but at least we touched base and knew that all was OK at home. Tomorrow we get propane and move on to Évora.

Miles in Lisbon (back and forth shopping): 95 Odom: 2882

May 30th:

Left camp at 8:30 and all headed to the propane plant. The traffic at the plant was heavy and slow. By the time the last of our group was filled up it was 11:40. We were among the last to leave because Hugh had been helping to direct the rigs onto the scales. Today we traveled alone and rolled right to Évora. We were actually the first ones in camp, a rarity. We got our laundry done and I cooked meat for dinner with enough left for another meal.

Miles today: 108 Odom: 2990

May 31st:

At 8:30 we were on our way again. We traveled with Betty and Larry Peters. It was a leisurely day and we just followed the log, no side trips. We found a wide parking area along the road in the village of Ervidel and stopped for a coffee break. There was a large building with green doors at the site and suddenly the doors opened. A group of ladies came out wondering who, what and why we were there. Good old charades…it was quickly established that we were American travelers and that they were cleaning the hall for a dance to be held on Saturday. We were invited to come back and enjoy the party. It was truly amazing to be able to communicate so much without even knowing the language. I grabbed my camera and asked them to let me take their photo and they happily complied. I promised them a copy and one lady gave me an address. I really did send them a copy when I got home in October

We found a delightful lunch stop beside a river in Odemira. We were able to park both our vans on the stone landing, put up our awnings, set up chairs and a folding table and have a leisurely lunch with friends, out in the fresh air.

We took an "ice cream" break at the harbor in Lagos and then headed for camp via Portimão. Portimão was a zoo with heavy traffic and a beach cluttered with high-rise housing. The park at Quarteira was OK but it was a little difficult to get the vehicles level. It was already late in the day so not being near the beach was not the disappointment it could have been.

Miles today: 194 Odom: 3184

Chapter 6 ~ Back to Spain

June 1st:

Another day on the road heading for Seville We got a late start and had a lazy day. We bought oranges, visited a Roman ruin, but it was hot so we didn't do too much walking. The campground, Villsom-Seville was easy to find, arrival time was 5:30. The view of Seville was beautiful but we had no great desire to go down into the town. We could see the Alhambra but I couldn't get a good photo. The heat made us all feel a little lethargic and no one was outside doing push-ups. Air-conditioning would have been welcomed.

Miles today: 158 Odom: 3342 Temperature: 106F

June 2nd:

It was a do nothing day, just too hot. We did get laundry done and dried it on clotheslines on the roof of the camp office. There were orange trees all around us but the oranges were not good for eating, too sour. However, in the courtyard in front of the camp office there was a huge lemon tree loaded with large, ripe lemons. When you "accidentally" bumped into the tree at least a half dozen lemons would fall at your feet. We made a LOT of lemonade. We met an Englishman in the park who wanted to buy a Lone Star belt buckle. No one had one but we did get his address and sent him one when we got back to the USA. We ate an early supper, took a cool shower and retired at 10.

June 3rd:

Today we were able to wash the vehicle for 80 pasetas and then meander to the next camp. We exchanged money for more pasetas and bought gas. We were the last ones out of camp and evidently didn't take any side trips or stop at any special scenic spot because we were the first ones to reach Puerto Real. We never wanted to appear to be eager beavers to get to camp first. Another couple had already earned that reputation, so we went out to dinner and "arrived" a little later.

Miles today: 103 Odom: 3445

Drivers meeting tonight! Tomorrow, off on the road to Morocco! (Reminds me of Bing Crosby and Bob Hope!)

Chapter 7 ~ North Africa & Gibraltar

June 4th:

8a.m. was departure time and we all left in rapid succession for the port of Algeciras. It was cool, windy and foggy almost all the way. The sun finally broke through when we reached the coast. We lined up on the ferry dock and, while there, we got the news that one of our group had dropped off the tour to head home because of family problems. It was sad to see them go when we had come this far.

Photo #10 ~ Ferry to Tangiers

The ferry trip lasted about three hours; the crossing was a little rough, the weather windy and cool. We gained two hours on the trip causing a little confusion.

Our Moroccan guide, Mohammed, met us at the pier. When we arrived at camp, a welcome committee of dancers and drummers greeted us and we were served tall glasses of mint tea. It was a whole different world.

Photo #11 ~ Welcome to Tangiers

We had our introduction to camels today. They smell and they spit. It's an experience to get on and off and I really did it.

Photo #12 ~ Camel Ride

Tomorrow we tour the Kasbah. We will follow that up with a Moroccan dinner and entertainment by a belly dancer. Who could ask for anything more? Tonight we are just tired.

Miles today: 75 Odom: 3520

June 5th:

A busy day with a city tour of Tangiers including the Kasbah. Our guide, Muhammad, herded us through the narrow alleys and recommended one shop in particular. It was very expensive and the owners and Muhammad were very well acquainted, possibly even relatives? I had more fun trading at the camp store and got a better deal. But to be in Tangiers and not see the Kasbah would be unthinkable. I can still hear the French actor, Charles Boyer, with his French accent and his hooded eyes saying, "Come with me to the Kasbah." Okay Charlie, I made it, where were you?

Dinner was good and the belly dancer was...limber? I can't imagine being that loose jointed. One point that stuck in my mind about this camp was being questioned by one of the young workers about the bible. He asked me if I had one to give him. Of course, even if I had been carrying one in the vehicle I wouldn't have given it to him. I did offer to send him one when I got back home but he definitely did not want to have one mailed to him. I still wonder what his purpose was. Was he possibly interested in Christianity or did he want to satisfy himself that his faith was better?

June 6th:

Today was another free day. Did the usual chores and repacked a lot of stuff. We all planned to go to dinner, Dutch treat tonight, so there will be no need to heat up the vehicles by cooking. We will leave Tangiers early in the morning. There will be a drivers meeting at 8 and departure at 8:30.

June 7th:

From Tangiers we drove down the Atlantic coast of Africa to Asilah. Asilah is an old walled town, much cleaner and more open than the Kasbah. It just isn't as colorful.

Lunch break gave Hugh a chance to nap; he didn't feel well. After lunch I drove the long haul over the Atlas mountain range. Slo'-Pokers® took a break at Medina to explore and shop. We stayed in our parked rig and relaxed. We were told later that Mohammad had rushed them through, led them to a restaurant of his choosing and a rug shop belonging to a relative. We were better off just resting in the car and watching the world go by. One of our fellow Slo'-Pokers® gave me some grief because he thought I had driven over the mountain too slowly holding him up. The fact that I was behind 3 huge trucks with no chance to pass didn't seem to matter. I politely told him what I thought of him and his attitude.

We actually became friends before the trip ended. I don't think any woman had ever stood up to him before.

When we left Medina we had crossed over the mountains and were headed downhill. The camp we headed to was actually an old camel caravan stop-over. There was no water, only outhouses, no level ground but a great view of the Mediterranean Sea. In spite of the lack of extra creature comforts it was very relaxing. We arrived here at 4:30 after a 108-mile drive. Tomorrow Gibraltar.

Miles today: 108 Odom: 3628

June 8th:

The trip to Gibraltar was smooth. The Spanish customs in Morocco were slow, but the boat was clean. We were amazed at Gibraltar. I had never dreamed that there would be such a large, busy city on the rock. The airport runway crossed a main highway so when a plane was moving along the runway the highway got a red light. It seemed so weird to be sitting at a traffic light while a large plane crossed the road in front of you.

Our parking spot was on top of the rock at the lighthouse. The view was magnificent but we were not allowed to spend the second night although, in the past, other Slo'-Poke Caravans® had been allowed to do so. The management had changed and so had the rules. As a result we planned to leave Gibraltar in the morning and find a campground in Spain.

We had driven 30 miles on Gibraltar. Odom 3658

Photo #13 ~ Camped on the Rock

Chapter 8 ~ Spain, Andorra, France and Monaco

June 9th:

We left the fabled rock and headed to a new campground "Camping Mabello Playa." It was a beautiful, immaculate park. We arrived at 4 p.m. after a 57-mile drive. We had the opportunity to get our vehicle washed, have an easy supper and take a walk through the park, all that and a good nights sleep.

Miles from Gibraltar: 57 Odom 3715

June 10th:

It was hard to leave peaceful, clean and quiet Camping Mabello Playa in the morning so we dawdled and took our time heading out. On the road to Grenada we had rain and our freshly washed van was filthy. The roads were slick and we almost got side-swiped when two vehicles skidded and collided on the road in front of us. We arrived in Grenada at 3 p.m.

Miles today: 110 Odom: 3825

June 11th:

Today was a quiet day in camp. Hugh helped Jim fix Arnold's refrigerator and then they pulled ours and fixed the pump. After lunch we took a break and drove to town. We visited the cathedral but everything else was closed so we headed back to camp.

June 12th:

Sunday prayer service was held at 8 a.m. and a drivers meeting at 8:15.

Most of the group left soon after. We washed our vehicle again and were the last ones out of the park at 9:18. About an hour later we caught up with Peters and traveled the rest of the route with them. An inviting little restaurant was a place to take a break and get a good meal. Further down the road we dawdled a little more to explore an abandoned cave dwelling, finally arriving at Santa Pola at 5:30 p.m.

Miles today: 225 Odom: 4050

June 13th:

Santa Pola was right on the beach so most of us got a chance to do some swimming. The day included a trip to the Super Continente market, and of course, washing a load of laundry. At least we had warm water and washing machines. After doing the wash by hand, in cold water, in cement tubs, outdoors, in 40 degree temperatures, in Holland, this was a piece of cake.

The sunshine and warm breeze got everything dry in a jiffy.

Our round trip to the market: 28 miles Odom: 4078.

June 14th:

An early start today for the propane plant. Once our tank was filled, we took a leisurely trip through beautiful mountains. We had seen signs for a supermarket but we missed it. We stayed in a rest area on the Autopista for the night.

Miles today: 237 Odom: 4315

June 15th:

At 8 a.m. we were back on the road. Paid two tolls on the Autopista -640pasetas and 55pasetas. The picturesque scenery in the Pyrenees made it all worthwhile. After 167 beautiful miles we pulled into our next campsite in Sant Julie de Loria, Andorra at 2 p.m.

Odom: 4482

June 16th:

Andorra is awesome. The mountains and hidden valleys at every turn made me happy that I was in the co pilot seat and could rubberneck. Poor Hugh had to keep his eyes on the road while I soaked up the scenery, but our pleasure was slightly marred by rain. Shopping in the supermarket was great. We bought an entire wheel of Edam cheese for very little money and I found the neatest stainless steel oilcan for a song. Now, many years later, it's still my olive oil dispenser.

Two months without a perm was beginning to show so I made some inquiries and took myself into town for a perm. The languages in Andorra are Spanish and French. Having only a smattering of highs school Spanish, it was back to charades. It was quite an experience, the owner of the shop was a young man; he directed the whole project and three young women apprentices did all the work. I was shampooed and pampered beyond anything I have ever received in a beauty parlor at home. The end result was a great perm for a very modest price.

June 17th:

One more day to shop and explore in Andorra. It was still raining but we had a nice surprise this morning. Our tour leaders served us a touch of home—a McDonalds breakfast!!! Yes, the Golden Arches were also in Andorra. Hugh and I shopped for gifts for our kids. We were able to purchase genuine Swiss army knives for our sons at amazingly low cost and other goodies for the girls and grand kids.

June 18th:

Spent our last day in Andorra in the rain but we still loved the place. Everyone had awnings out and we managed a potluck supper and farewell party for the Scotts. Their departure from the tour had been pre-planned.

Back and forth in Andorra we drove 25 miles, Odom: 4507.

Photo #14 ~ Village in Andorra

June 19th:

Today we crossed back into France. The highway out of Andorra was full of switchbacks and curves and the weather was foggy, windy, rainy and we even had a little sleet. There was a fair amount of truck traffic and the going was slow but the scenery was fantastic. We passed one village nestled off the highway that, like all of Andorra, was tidy, compact and lovely.

En route to Porto Barcares we stopped in a walled town, Ville Franche, to sight-see and take pictures. We arrived at our camp in Porto Barcares at 2:15 and to our delight, we had hot dishwater and washing machines. It's amazing that the things you take for granted at home become a luxury.

Miles today: 126 Odom: 4646

June 19th:

(Father's Day) Fortunately, we traveled alone today. We got lost in Montpelier and we got lost in Aix-en-Provence (affectionately known as aches in the province). We finally got it all straightened out but were happy that we had not misguided anyone else. It was one of those days where nothing seemed to go right. We made it to camp at 4:30 p.m.

Mileage today: 216 Odom: 4862

June 20th:

We had a free day and took advantage by exploring. We drove through the hill country north of Aix to Apt. It was a relaxing day and we enjoyed the leisurely travel. We took a lunch break in a nice roadside pull-off and gradually meandered back to our camp.

Drove 34 miles today. Odom: 4896

June 21st:

Today we are scheduled to reach the, much touted, Riviera. We traveled towards Port Grimaud via the Grand Canyon of Verdun. The canyon was a great experience, full of winding roads and awesome scenery. Our arrival at Port Grimaud was something else. The camping area was crowded and noisy, a real suburbia. The "scenery" left much to be desired. Close to 100% of the campers were bare topped. The men weren't too bad some of the females (from little girls to grandmothers) were not attractive. Pendulous, sagging breasts, bulging bellies and wide bottoms crammed into tiny bikinis can't possibly compete with Keukenhof flower gardens or ancient roman arches as feasts for the eye.

June 22nd:

Once our laundry was done we took the ferry to St. Tropez. It was interesting for an hour or so but much too expensive—just not our place.

We leave tomorrow.

Odom: 5147

June 23rd:

At 9:15 a.m. we left on our own with plans to reconnect with the group at Ventimiglia on the 25th. It was a very peaceful day with a stop for lunch at a Sodim supermarket cafeteria and a stop in Nice to get cash. In Eze (pronounced eezay) we found a wonderful campground for the night atop the Grand Corniche. It was still misty but we hoped for a clear a.m. because the view was reported to be spectacular. Tomorrow we will visit the village of Eze and Monte Carlo. The food in the park restaurant was excellent and we planned breakfast there in the morning.

Only 100 miles today. Odom: 5247

June 24th:

After a really delicious breakfast we visited the village of Eze. Met the Peters; they had just arrived in Eze. They had left the group at 6 a.m. and taken the Autopista. On leaving Eze we got into heavy traffic and drove through Monaco without stopping to explore. Traffic was so slow that a lady walking with a cane passed us every time we stopped for a stop light. When the light turned green we would pass her, only to see her pass us again at the next light. The comedy was repeated three more times. This was the great point of interest in Monaco. Some people would have visited the casino or the palace but not us; we raced a lady with a cane (and lost).

Chapter 9 ~ Italy

We reached the Italian border at 12:30. The Auto Club (like AAA) was closed for lunch. We had to buy our gas discount tickets from them so we parked and ate our lunch. Once we had our tickets we headed to camp arriving at 2 p.m. For dinner we were treated to a REAL Italian dinner…Spaghetti, and so began the Italian part of our Odyssey.

Miles today: 26 Odom: 5273

June 25th:

At 8:30 a.m. we left the Ventimiglia campground, went into to town to cash travelers checks for Liras. Hugh waited in the car while I went into the bank and when I headed back to the car I was run over—by a bicycle. The cyclist came zooming around the corner and knocked me down and then proceeded to rant at me. He didn't even offer to help me up; some kind bystanders did that. I had some beautiful bruises and was physically sore but mentally I was steaming. What we referred to as the "Ventimiglia incident" was a poor way to start our visit to Italy, but we had high hopes.

Pisa was our next destination. We got on the Autostrada that follows the coast. It is an amazing feat of engineering. The coast is a series of inlets and cliffs down to the water and as a result the highway consists of many tunnels and bridges. It is either tunneling through a mountain or crossing a cove, very picturesque. The European super highways lack the bumps and frost heaves that we so often find on our thruways at home.

Arrived at camp in Pisa at 3 p.m. It was still early in the day so we took the short walk into town. We saw the cathedral and the leaning tower. As often as we had seen pictures of the leaning tower, it was fascinating to see the real thing. There was a festival going on in town, involving the Italian Red Cross. A military band was playing right in front of the leaning tower. We obviously had arrived in Pisa at a special time. We learned that there would be more festivities in town the following day.

Our toll on the Autostrada for just under 200 miles was 31500 Lira which came to $24.40 ($.12 per mile).

Miles today: 201 Odom: 5474

June 26th:

An unforgettable day. The celebration in Pisa, *Gioco del Ponte* (Game of the Bridge) was one of the most entertaining events we ever attended. It dates back to medieval times and is as colorful. The parade consists of hundreds of costumed warriors wearing real or reproductions of medieval or renaissance battle gear. Most carry *mazzascudos* (club shield), weapons originally used in the 11th century. The actual contest takes place on the bridge crossing the Arno River and is between teams from both sides of the river, Tramontana and Mezzogiorno. Teams from the town's four quarters try to push a rail-mounted, seven-ton trolley over the main bridge and into the other team's territory.

When we arrived at the riverside, people were standing ten deep and it was impossible to see anything. There were bleachers set up which afforded a great view. Hugh, again in his best Italian, asked about buying seats and was told by the usher that they were all sold out long ago. Leave it to Hugh to find a way. He happened to have a photo in his wallet of himself in a foxhole in Italy during the war. He was carrying it because he hoped to connect with an Italian family he had befriended while in an encampment near Certaldo. He showed the usher the picture and told him he had heard of this event while in Italy and had hoped that he might be able to visit Pisa after the war and actually attend. I don't know if it was the picture of a weary soldier or his big blue eyes, we wound up in second row seats in the bleachers. We were only seated a few moments when someone tapped us on the shoulder and our first thought was "Oh, oh, we must be in someone's seat." It was a man behind us offering us the use of his binoculars. We quickly learned that we were among people who were routing for the team Tramontana. Of course, we too shouted "Tramontana" whenever they did.

47

Photo #15 & #16 ~ Games of the Bridge

There were several other couples from the Slo'-Poke Caravan®
that had come to see the show. Unfortunately they were standing in
the crowd and couldn't see much. They did not miss the fact that we

were in the bleachers. One of our fellow travelers commented later to Hugh that his respect for Hugh had grown dramatically because Hugh had managed to get us seats when no seats were available. It seemed a poor reason to "respect" anyone. If it was supposed to be a complement it failed.

We did have a small price to pay; without sun-block we both had quite a sun burn but it was worth it. I will always remember Pisa as a highlight of the journey for the pageantry and the friendliness of the people.

June 27th:

Said goodbye to Pisa at 8:30 and headed for Venice via the Autostrada.

We used the last of our discount gas tickets today. Our total gas cost for the 220-mile drive was 26100 Lira.

We were in camp by 3 p.m. Odom: 5694 and headed into Venice by bus. We took a motorboat taxi to St. Marks Square, visited the Doge's Palace, explored and took photos and then walked back to the bus depot. It was a long, long walk but we stopped for supper at a sidewalk café and did a little shopping. We got back to camp at 9 p.m. Tomorrow, we leave the caravan and head for San Marino and Certaldo. We will rejoin the group in Florence.

Chapter 10 ~ The Search

June 28th:

A new adventure, on our own, began at 9a.m. when we started the run to San Marino and Certaldo. We got pretty snarled up in Mestre but then found our way. We stopped at a farm stand and bought fresh fruit. There was a wide enough space for us to park and enjoy our lunch. The weather was partly cloudy with intermittent showers.

San Marino is a fascinating principality on top of a mountain. Unfortunately it rained enough that we didn't get any good pictures but the shopping was great. Everything was very inexpensive. We spent a couple of hours just exploring and then headed back down the mountain. It was the only time in our lives that we looked down on a rainbow. There were showers and sunshine in the valley as we descended the mountain and the rainbow was actually below us.

We followed the coastal highway southward to Fano and turned off to head west towards Florence The S3 highway was an awesome road with lots of tunnels; one was almost 2 miles long. There was no shoulder where we could pull off and we began to worry about driving well after dark before finding a place to stop.

Then, suddenly we spotted a camp symbol and pulled in. The road was long and ended on a waterfront but it was pretty, quiet and clean. We had a good supper, nice hot showers and a good nights' sleep.

Miles today: 238 Odom: 5932

June 29th:

As we were checking out in the morning, the owner, who spoke English, chatted with us a while. When Hugh told him we were heading for Certaldo to look up friends he had made during the war, he shook Hugh's hand and thanked him for his service during the war.

We visited the walled town of Gubbio and then looked for the scenic route to Perugia. Of course, we got lost but prevailed and found the way. The route was truly scenic. We stopped for lunch in a very nice restaurant in Petrignano. The waitress was a little stunned when all we ordered was ravioli since pasta is only one course in a good Italian meal. But the ravioli was so good and the portion was so large that we were quite content to break tradition.

Our next stop along the historic highway was Assisi. We spent some time in the church and visited the tomb of St. Francis. Showers continued throughout the day, but Assisi was a special place, one I will always remember.

We did not make a stop in Perugia because we wanted to get a little closer to Certaldo before stopping for the night. We found a good campsite in Siena, had a leisurely supper and took a walk before settling in for the night.

In the morning I struck up a conversation with the woman in the next campsite. She had presumed that we were German because our camper had German travel markers. Like so many, she had a sad WWII story to tell. Her father was a German soldier. When she was four years old he had a brief visit home at Christmas. He was very depressed as the war dragged on and on and told his family if it continued much longer he would "make tracks." He returned to duty in Italy and, while on patrol, he disappeared. It was his habit to smoke his pipe and cut himself a walking stick when he was on patrol. When he didn't return from patrol his unit searched for him and found his pipe and his walking stick but he was never found. The decision was that guerrilla fighters had caught him and, without a doubt, had killed him.

As she told me this story she assured me that her father had never come home and would have done so if it had been possible and that her mother was still waiting for him to come back. How many families have had no closure when their loved ones have just vanished?

Miles today: 141 Odom: 6073

June 30th:

At 8:50, our search to find the Mathis family really began in earnest. We went straight to Certaldo. When we arrived in the town we stopped in a hardware store and inquired about the Mathis family but no one knew them. Right on cue, the mail carrier arrived and the shopkeeper asked him if he knew anyone named Mathis. He said the Mathis family had moved to Colle Val d'Elsa. However, the first names of the Mathis' family he knew did not match the family Hugh knew. If they were relatives they might lead us to the right family so we headed for Colle Val d'Elsa.

As we approached the town center we quickly discovered it was "Market Day" The town center was filled with booths, tents, stalls, wagons and crowds everywhere. We couldn't stop to make inquiries so we continued on passed the market square. A short distance further we saw a building on the left side of the road that looked as though it might be an official building.

There were two policemen, armed with semi-automatic pistols, walking back and forth in front of the building. That convinced us that it was definitely "Official". While I might have hesitated, Hugh did not. Again, with his meager Italian vocabulary, he tried to communicate with the police. They were quick to realize that we were American (or English). The one that handled the role of spokesman said, "No Inglese." But he didn't just brush us off; he pointed to the building and said "Professore." That cleared up one question; the building was obviously a school. We entered the building and were met by a very attractive lady. She was a teacher and the school was a high school. She did not speak English but found a student who did. He was delighted to be able to practice his language skills and we were happy for the help. He looked up the Mathis family in the phone book and tried to call them, but no one was home. They were probably all at the market. We thanked the student, the teacher and the police officers and climbed back into our camper. Hugh was disappointed but he wasn't giving up. In the meantime he suggested we just roam a bit and then find our way back to Certaldo. The road we were on led to Volterra and was actually one along which Hugh

52

had plodded during the war. It was hilly country and the road had several sharp curves. As we rounded one of the right wending curves Hugh let out a shout, "There they are!" He found a wide spot and pulled over. He had often spoken of seeing skyscrapers in the hills of Tuscany and no one had believed him, but sure enough, there in the distance were skyscrapers. The sight didn't clear up the mystery but at least Hugh felt vindicated; he had not imagined their existence.

We proceeded to Volterra and decided we would not want to be there in an earthquake. The town is picturesque but appears to be sitting on the edge of a cliff, hence the name, Vol (to fly) Terra (land). When we left, we again headed for Certaldo. We came to a fork in the road and Hugh took the right. I looked at the map and saw that the left headed to Certaldo and suggested that he turn around and take the left road. I don't know what was leading us that day but Hugh said, "Which ever way the good Lord leads us is the way we'll go." Within minutes the mystery of the skyscrapers was solved, they were right in front of us. We had stumbled on the town of San Gimignano. The "sky scrapers" were actual towers and there were fewer than Hugh had seen in 1943.

The town is a pedestrian village with a fascinating history. Long ago a man in town grew wealthy so he built a tower next to his home. Soon someone got a little richer built a taller tower and so it continued until there were at least 40 towers. Through the centuries many have crumbled and fallen but it is still a sight to behold. The town itself is very picturesque. I took quite a few pictures but one special one was taken looking through an iron gate into a courtyard filled with plants and a stairway. The painting of that courtyard hangs on my wall today. We could have spent more time but were anxious to continue our search so we said goodbye to the town of towers.

We headed back to Certaldo, entering the town from a different direction than our previous attempt. We spotted a large building that looked like it might contain offices or, perhaps, the library. As Hugh was parking he commented that he wished he could find the street where the Mathis family had lived, Via Cavour. When he got out of our van, he walked to the corner and looked at the street sign…it was Via Cavour. I waited while he walked up the street looking for the house. He came back shaking his head. The house was no longer there; the space where it had stood now held a bell tower for an adjoining church. Now, more than ever, Hugh felt we were closing in and would find the Mathis family. We entered the front door of the building on the corner, hoping to find someone that could help us. The hallway had several closed doors but at the end of the hall was an open door to a brightly lit room.

By now we were "psyched" and walked right in. To our embarrassment we found ourselves <u>behind</u> the counter in the police station. To say the least, we created quite a commotion. The proper entrance to the station was at the back of the building. We quickly moved around to the other side of the counter. I can only describe what happened next as a typical Italian comedy. Everyone began talking at once, loudly! The man in charge was large and had a commanding voice. Hugh tried desperately to make himself understood, trying to explain that we were looking for the Mathis family. The big man realized that we couldn't really speak Italian and he couldn't speak English so he sent for two young women from another office that "could speak English!" They arrived smiling sweetly and their knowledge of English was refreshing. They knew how to say, "Hello, goodbye, please, and thank you very much."

While all this was going on several cops came off their beat and wandered in to watch the fun.

We were getting pretty disillusioned and about ready to give it up when one of the cops that had been behind the counter and on the phone suddenly came to us with information. He had been busy while the comic opera was going on and he told us that the Mathis daughters both lived in Florence, one married to a professor named Crocca and their address was #1 Via Beltrami. At last we had information and our next stop was Florence.

We thanked everyone profusely (in loud voices!) and left immediately to rejoin our tour in Florence. When we checked in at the campground we were happy to find that the camp personnel spoke English. We asked the lady at the desk how we could get to Via Beltrami.

Our bubble of anticipation was promptly punctured when; after looking at a city directory and a phone book, she declared there was no Via Beltrami in Florence nor was there a family named Crocca in the phone book.

We set up our camp and Hugh went to the camp store to buy a map of Florence. He was sure that he could find Via Beltrami on the map. He spread the map out on a large flat surface and began his search. The lady shopkeeper wanted to know for what he was searching and he told her, " Via Beltrami."

She promptly joined him in the search. The bread deliveryman arrived and wanted to know what they were looking for. Once they told him, he put down the rack of bread and joined them at the table. The same thing happened with the CocaCola man, the newspaperman and several others. Everyone surrounded the map and eventually Hugh was standing outside the ring. Of course they were all talking loudly and gesturing but the final verdict was that, indeed , there was no Via Beltrami in Florence. When Hugh returned to our campsite he had made a resolution. We would take a bus into Florence in the morning, locate a hall of records and continue the search.

We joined Caravan group activities that evening but opted out of the next days planned sightseeing to continue our quest.

Miles today: 152 Odom: 6225

Chapter 11 ~ Reunion

July 1st:

It was time to make one more try to connect with the Mathis daughters.

We were heading towards the gate en route to the bus stop when a man from the camp office called to us, "I found them!" and I don't know how but he had really "found them." It was all a matter of a few letters; the street was Via Bertani and the family name was Accrocca. He gave us specific bus instructions and away we went. We asked the bus driver to let us know when to get off the bus and he graciously did. He pointed us to Via Bertani which was just a few steps from the bus stop. The first building was the #1 we were looking for. We entered the lobby and there on one of the mailboxes were the names Mathis/Accrocca. We rang the bell and the door was buzzed open. When we stepped in a man and a young woman were half-way down the stairs and Hugh said "Tina Mathis?" The both answered, "Si, Si". Hugh took out a letter we had received from Tina's father after Hugh got home from Italy and handed it to them. The young women looked at it and said, in perfect English, "How did get a letter from my grandfather?" We had found them!

Hugh showed them the photo of him in the foxhole and we were invited up to the apartment. Tina was probably resting since it was past lunchtime, but her daughter went in and soon she appeared. She took one look at Hugh and said "Oh signore Ugo!" and a lot more. Her daughter interpreted for us, and her husband Aldo just smiled. Apparently, since Tina was a little girl when she met Hugh she probably associated him with people of her father's age and, having lost her father a few years earlier, it was hard for her to realize that Hugh was not long dead.

We did not want to impose so suddenly so plans were made for us to come to dinner the following day. Tina's sister lived just around the corner and would also be there. Aldo was not a professor; he was a doctor. The daughter, Emilia, was the professor, a Russian translator.

Hugh was on cloud nine. He had found his wonderful Italian family that had welcomed the soldiers so many years before. We looked forward to the next day when we would have hours to spend with them.

July 2nd:

We started from camp early enough to buy flowers for our hostess.

When we were ringing the doorbell, Tina's sister Josephine arrived, carrying a covered dish for the luncheon. It was another great re-union. We enjoyed a lovely meal and all managed to communicate in spite of the language barrier. Hugh managed with the Italian he had learned while stationed in Italy; I managed with charades as did Aldo and the sisters. I found out that Aldo loved music, especially popular show tunes from great American musicals.
He had a rack with an amazing collection of cassettes and we soon discovered that we had a common bond in music.

After the luncheon we all piled into Aldo's small car to go touring to the place where Hugh had once been encamped. I'm not sure that everyone appreciated it but Aldo and I sang a lot of the hit tunes from the great musicals. Of course our lyrics consisted primarily of "lah-da-da."

For Hugh the revisit to his old bivouac and to the little house where the Mathis family had camped during the war was a nostalgic experience.
We spent some time at the little house and Hugh pointed out the fig trees where Tina and Josephine had conned him into stealing ripe figs for them.
We stopped in Certaldo for ice cream and did some more sightseeing and ended up the tour with great thin crust pizza.

Photo #17 ~ Site of WW II Bivouac

It was getting late and our hosts drove us back to camp where we said good-bye. We were scheduled to leave for Rome in the morning. We really hated to leave them and, surprisingly, it was Aldo who had tears in his eyes when we parted.

Miles since Siena: 152 Odom: 6225

July 3rd:

Our 47th wedding anniversary! We bid the hills of Tuscany goodbye and headed on to Rome. Our actual camp was in Prima Porta outside of Rome. But we were close to the railroad so it was possible to go to Rome without taking our vans into the city. The thing that touched us the most in this campground was the busload of Polish pilgrims, in town to see fellow son of Poland, Pope John Paul II.

Their encampment consisted of tents only; they were obviously not wealthy but the warmth and friendship this group extended to us was wonderful. We were invited to their campfire, offered some homemade liquid fire, toasted and serenaded for our anniversary and spent the evening humming along to their music.

The campground was situated on the banks of the Tiber and our log contained the following warning: **"It is so contaminated, do not drink, swim or even put your foot or hand in if you have a scratch."** That killed any foolish yen we may have had to go skinny-dipping in the Tiber.

Miles today: 160 Odom: 6385

July 4th:

Independence Day! Hugh stuck a small flag in the band of his hat and we enjoyed a bus tour of Rome. (I still have that little flag!). Among the many famous sites in Rome we visited the Coliseum, Pantheon, Spanish Steps, Vittorio EmanueleII Memorial (nicknamed the Wedding Cake) and, of course, the Trevi Fountain. We all threw coins in the fountain and I'm sure I wasn't the only one to have the tune "Three Coins in the Fountain" running through may head for the remainder of the day.

We had been warned about small groups of young children surrounding us, presumably to sell papers. Actually it was a pickpocket scam and it did happen to Betty and Larry Peters. They found themselves alone in a small square when several children approached them, chattering away and waving a newspaper. Betty and Larry kept shaking their heads and saying "No" when something dropped at Larry's feet. It was his wallet. He quickly put his foot on it and the children scattered. A tiny little girl, with delicate fingers, had slid it right out of his trouser pocket and he never felt it go. If she hadn't dropped it he would never have known that it was gone until much later. That's the other side of Rome.

We had some time to explore on our own in Rome and we also had and audience with the Holy Father, Pope John Paul II. The line outside the hall was long and everyone wanted to be first. I have never been shoved, pushed and elbowed as much as I was on that line, and this by my fellow Christians.

The audience hall was filled to capacity and His Holiness addressed the crowd in seven different languages. He acknowledged us as the Pilgrims from Florida and our Polish friends stood and serenaded him in their native tongue.

In another building, across from the large assembly hall, public lavatories were available. Hugh and I both headed in, ladies to the left, gents to the right. That restroom matron was a real dragon. There was an empty chair in the waiting area and after Hugh had given a very generous donation to her dish he sat down to wait for me. The dragon had a fit and told him he had to leave. Of course he wouldn't leave without me so fortunately I was prompt.

The dragon was still sputtering and by now Hugh had his Irish up. He retrieved his generous donation and plunked the smallest coin he had and we walked out.

It was hot in the city and we stopped twice to buy bottles of water to quench our thirst. We had a great lunch in a restaurant near the train station. One of the waiters spoke English and we chatted with him until their regular crowd arrived and he got busy. The train dropped us right near our camp and we made preparations to leave in the morning for Pompeii. Our Polish friends were packing up to board their bus for home. We got the address of two and kept in touch at Christmas for years to come.

July 7th:

It was Arrividerci Roma. At 8:30 we rolled out of the park headed for Naples with an en route stop at Pompeii We loafed our way down the Appian way, visited the ruins and continued on to Naples. We parked at the ferry pier and got some exercise just walking around the pier and chatting with our fellow travelers. We packed the necessities for the day trip to Capri, cameras, snacks and cash, then settled in for the night.

Miles today: 185 Odom: 6570

July 8th:

The weather was perfect for the trip to Capri. What a beautiful place; no wonder it has inspired songs. The panoramas were extraordinary. We took lots of pictures and did some shopping. We each bought a wonderful straw hat (I still have mine) and some nice souvenirs for the family. We took a boat trip around the island to view the blue grotto and hated to leave the little paradise. It was a rare day and we hoped to return some day but we still had places to go and things to see so we bid Capri farewell.

On our return to camp we found out that our boat to Yugoslavia would be sailing from Ancona at midnight, not from Pescara as originally planned With the additional miles involved we planned an early start.

Chapter 12 ~ Eastward

July 9th:

We hit the road at 7:30, filled our propane tank and headed across the mountains towards Ancona. We took a short break at a little grocery store to buy bread and had a lengthy conversation with the owner. He had lived in Ohio for 20 years but his English was still about as good as Hugh's Italian. Finally, at 6 p.m., we arrived at the pier in Ancona. We sat on the pier until we were finally boarded on the *Tiziano* at 10: p.m.

Miles today: 304 Odom: 6874

It was a long, uncomfortable, night. With a father and a brother that spent their lives at sea as captains, I'm almost embarrassed to admit that I am not always comfortable at sea.

July 10th:

We docked at Split, Yugoslavia and drove to our camp at 11 a.m. After lunch I took a long nap and after supper I took a nice hot shower and crawled right into bed.

July 11th:

Evidently I made up for the sleep lost during the crossing from Italy. Jim and Hugh went by bus to get gas coupons while I did laundry and hauled out the rig, got things shipshape again. The last week had been so busy that we hadn't taken much time for chores. Happily the little restaurant in the camp was good so we dined out. The camp was crowded but friendly and clean.

Mileage from pier to camp: 3 Odom: 6877

July 12th:

Began the run to Dubrovnik at 8:00a.m. arriving at Kupari without incident. Camp facilities were filthy; quite a letdown after Split. We wondered, "Is this an example of what it's like to live under the banner of the hammer and sickle?" There was a military presence in the camp and a strong sense of "unfriendliness." It was too hot to go city touring but thankfully the night was cooler so we could sleep.

Miles today: 145 Odom: 7022

July 13th:

My only note for this date is that we had a birthday party for our leader, Jim Hayden. With no further comment in my log, I can only assume that I was not enthralled with Kupari.

July 14th:

At 8:15 we left Kupari with pleasure and headed for Titograd. The scenery along coastal road and through the mountains was wonderful. We stopped in a small mountaintop cafe for lunch. The owner was friendly and helpful. He managed to explain the menu and we chose fresh caught trout for lunch. We arrived at a quiet camp in Titograd at 3 p.m.

The whole day was a pleasure and ended with a good nights sleep.

Miles today: 125 Odom: 7147

July 15th:

This day, although the scenery was spectacular, hit a sour note. We saw a young man (probably late teenager) hitchhiking and foolishly gave him a lift. He was very pleasant and polite and we managed to communicate with the usual charades. When we reached a place called Rozaj he indicated that he wanted to get out. He thanked us profusely and we were happy to have connected with a local person. Ten miles down the road there was an interesting view and I reached back for the binoculars, only to find that they had left the vehicle with our hitchhiker.

It turned out to be "one of those days." The route now was hilly and full of curves but the views were awesome so we took our time. We loafed along enjoying the easy pace and the scenery. We entered a village and were stopped by what we presumed to be, a police officer. He informed us that we had been speeding going 70k in a 60k stretch. We were puzzled because it certainly was not true. We assumed that he was confusing us with one of our other Slo'-Poker® vans since we all looked alike. But this guy was adamant; he kept saying "radar" and he indicated that our fine of heaven knows what was due on the spot. We had brief visions of languishing in a Yugoslavian prison because we had very little of their currency. Amazingly $2.00 US satisfied the fee. Was that a racket or was that a racket? It was not the money that got my dander up, it was the principle. If Hugh hadn't shot me a warning look I might have lost my cool and told that little toad off.

We continued along the scenic road and stopped where 2 little girls were selling hand woven bags. Of course they didn't speak English. When I showed interest in one bag they couldn't tell me what I should pay so they motioned us up to the house. Their father, a tall solemn man, tried to give us a quote but we couldn't understand it. I took a $5 bill and offered it. That was evidently more than satisfactory because he accepted it, motioned to the girls and they politely showed us out.

We finally arrived at Skopje at 6 p.m, spent a quiet evening and early to bed.
Tomorrow Greece!

Miles today: 240 Odom: 7387

July 16th:

At 8:30 we all bailed out of Skopje and headed south towards Greece.

At a rest area we all unloaded what Yugoslavian money we had on snacks.

We were surprised when he came to a tollbooth on the highway; this was an addition since Jim & Duby and had laid out the route. Now what? Would we be held in Yugoslavia forever? An American $1 bill put a big smile on the tollbooth attendant and we breezed right through. We got Drachmas and saw Mt. Olympus looming off to our right. It was awesome. As we neared Meteora we saw the huge rocks and cliffs but the heat was so overwhelming that we did not drive the loop. There was a swimming pool in the camp but it was so packed that it didn't beckon. I couldn't imagine trying to cool off standing shoulder to shoulder with dozens of other sweaty people.

Miles today: 255 Odom: 7662

July 17th:

With our journey half over we said goodbye to Meteora and headed to a beach camp at Stylis. We had a campsite close to the beach and there was a welcome breeze which made the heat more bearable. We actually romped around in the water for a while. We were scheduled to stay put for two days so we enjoyed a day of leisure on Sunday and a good nights rest. Monday we took care of essentials like an oil change and grocery shopping. We found a SUPER market…fresh cold cuts, iced tea mix, butter, bacon, cheese, baked beans; everyone went a little crazy in the market. Back at the camp this sweet Greek grandmother tried to speak with us. We did communicate after a fashion, you know—charades!

The restaurant in the camp was very good and the owners spoke good English. The young man that was managing the camp store was home on summer break from medical school in Georgia, USA. All in all the two days in Stylis were most enjoyable.

Mileage from Meteora: 99 Odom: 7761
Mileage in and around Stylis: 31 Odom: 7792

July 19th:

Left Stylis for Athens at 8:45 a.m. under a cloudy sky. We welcomed the slightly cooler air. The route to Athens took us through Delphi. We did some shopping but did not visit the ruins. I had been privileged to see them on a previous trip in 1974 during the "off" season when it wasn't crowded, but this was July and the place was crawling with tourists.

We made one more stop at Arachova. Our bus tour in 1974 had also stopped there and I will never forget it. It had been a long ride and I needed a rest room so I had approached our tour guide and asked if there was a public rest room anywhere. She asked me to wait while she made inquiries. She promptly returned and beckoned me to follow. We entered a shop that sold lots of hand woven articles and ushered me to the rear of the store. She told me to go behind the curtain and there it was… a marble slab with footprints and a hole over a gurgling brook! When in Rome…!

This time I was able to repay the use of their facility in 1974 by buying several shirts and a few other souvenirs.

At 3:30 we arrived at Camping Acropolis, Kifisia Crosssing, Attica, Greece.
A group headed out in the evening to see the Acropolis light show but we stayed in camp. I had been to the Acropolis and Hugh didn't really feel like going. We had gone to the light shows in Mexico at the Aztec ruins and both found it more interesting to wander through the ruins in daylight.

Miles today: 172 Odom: 7964

Our schedule for the rest of the week included free days on Wednesday and Friday, an island tour on Thursday and departure to Turkey on Saturday.

July 20th:

Hugh and I took off for Corinth to see the amazing Corinth canal. It was originally envisioned 825BC but was finally built in the

19th century. To be able to stand on the bridge crossing the canal and look into the chasm at vessels cruising below is an experience one never forgets.

Photo #18 ~ Amazing Corinth Canal

We saw the first Christian church established by the Apostle Paul. It was a real privilege to walk back into ancient history. In the scriptures we read so much of St. Paul, his conversion, his extensive travel and his teachings. To actually see the church he established left a deeper impression than many other sites.

The shopping was good in Corinth in a very modern super market. We thoroughly enjoyed our day. Every so often it was good to go it alone. Unfortunately, I got too busy sightseeing and shopping to keep up with logging mileage.

July 21st:

A perfect weather day for a tour of the Greek Islands. The ship was crowded but everyone aboard was filled with a holiday spirit. The islands are beautiful and it's easy to see why they are such a great tourist attraction. It would have been great fun to spend a week or two on any one of them. But we had miles and months to go and more wonderful things to see.

July 22nd:

Another day to roam on our own. We spent more time in Corinth, put in time doing laundry and tidying up the van. Tomorrow we head for Turkey.

July 23rd:

Hugh got drachmas from the camp manager so that he could go back to Corinth to pick up new sneakers and fill up with propane. At 2:45 we left for the port of Pireaus. One of our group had a vehicle break-down. We couldn't leave them stranded in Greece so they had to be towed. That really made life interesting. We had visions of all taking turns towing the disabled vehicle on and off ferries and over hill and dale for days to come.

Chapter 13 ~ Turkey

We had arrived at the dock at 3:30 and waited, and waited. We were finally loaded and sailed at 7:30. Because it was an overnight trip we were assigned cabins. Hugh and I shared with Betty and Larry Peters. I think the cabins were in the lowest possible deck and the walls were thin as paper. We could hear loud voices on the other side of the wall and lots of bumping and banging. The temperature, with four of us squeezed into a very tight space, rose to unbearable. I headed up to the lounge and read until midnight. I dozed a while and finally went back to bed at 2 a.m.

July 24th:

We landed at the island of Xios at 9 a.m., wandered around, had some lunch and awaited the ferry to Izmir. The ferry could only carry 4 or 5 vehicles so it was a slow process. At 5 p.m. we rolled into BP Mocamp at Inciralti-Izmir, Turkey.

July 25th:

The day was spent in camp. Hugh had an idea of what was wrong with the Stacey's van. He thought the problem was a faulty coil. To test that theory he removed the coil from our van and put it into the Stacey's van. The engine turned over and purred like a kitten. Problem solved…well not exactly. Obviously we had to find a replacement coil and it was a business holiday of some sort. However, Jim had an idea of where they might obtain a part. Mission accomplished. Our coil was put back and the Stacey's were independently mobile again. We all heaved a sigh of relief because there were higher elevations ahead and the thought of towing another van was not a happy one.

Miles since Athens: 179 Odom: 8143

July 26th:

The trip to Troy was interesting, especially the replica of the wooden horse (made of pressure treated lumber!). Enjoyed dinner in pretty nice restaurant; the snacks were fried cheese sticks that were delicious. The whole group was able to park in the lot at the Trojan Horse for the night.

Miles: 205 Odom: 8348

Photo #19 ~ Trojan Horse

July 27th:

At 9:15 we headed for Bursa. There were lots of vegetable stands along the way and everything was very inexpensive. Some of us bought potatoes, tomatoes and onions to split with others in the group. We were now dealing in Turkish liras so 500 liras for a kilo of tomatoes was downright cheap. It was also a lot of tomatoes! We arrived our camp in Bursa at 4:30 with enough time to freshen up, have supper and prepare for a city tour. Bursa at night was lovely. We had an opportunity to go to a real "Turkish Bath" and quite a few of the group did go. Hugh and I opted for a walking tour and some window-shopping; public bathing was just not our thing.

Tomorrow we leave for Istanbul.

Since Troy mileage: 315 Odom: 8563

From here on we will be heading westward; hard to realize that we have been on the road since April.

July 28th:

The run to Istanbul was an easy 156 mile; arrived at BP Mocamp at 2:15. Our mail was waiting for us, and there were letters for us from three of our children. Letters from home were always a treat.

We were scheduled to be in Istanbul until August 1st. The camp had a good restaurant that saved us the hassle of going grocery shopping. One of the waiters in the restaurant became our "friend". We spoke no Turkish and he spoke no English and yet we got along just fine. He was a great kidder, always bringing us a different wine than we ordered and grinning from ear to ear. We'd shake our head "No" and, with a flourish, he would produce the right bottle that he was holding behind his back. He wanted, very much, to come to the United States and actually wanted us to sponsor him. That was not something we could do since we had already sponsored our British son-in-law. His name was Nechate Barak and I often wonder what became of him.

July 29th:

Was a free day and we tended to chores and loafed. We had been warned to never leave our vehicle unlocked, even for a moment. Our log had the following notation in capital bold print: <u>YOU WON'T EVEN THINK ABOUT DRIVING INTO TOWN WILL YOU,</u> so we didn't.

July 30th:

We had an all day boat trip on the Bosporus that was very enjoyable. It was a small boat and only Slo'-Poke® members were on board. The weather was ideal for the trip and both sides of the river were fascinating. There were huge estates along the way. We made a stop ashore for an hour for tea and pastry and a few souvenirs. Then we continued to a point near the Black Sea for lunch. On our return to Istanbul we visited the Spice market and the Grand Bazaar. Both places were crowded and amazing, not just for what was available but for the history.

Photo #19-B ~ Istanbul

Before the time of Christ, when Turkey was known as Trace, it was a great market center where East and West met. The Grand Bazaar was built, by order of Mehmed II in the 15th century. There have been many changes through the passing centuries but it is still an incredible collection of hundreds of shops, all under one roof.

We also visited the Blue Mosque, which is built over the ruins of a large Christian church. Several things about the mosque I found surprising: the floor is ankle deep in carpets and how they deal with shoes. Everyone was required to remove shoes, which would be returned to us upon exiting. Our group alone numbered over forty people and yet when we exited the mosque we were all handed the correct pair of shoes. How do they do that?

July 31st:

We had a half-day trip into Istanbul with a stop at Topkapi Palace. The lavish displays of jewelry and artifacts and the structure of the palace itself were true marvels. All in all, our visit to Istanbul brought a lot of history to life for us. Things we had read about and seen pictures of in a history book so long ago were now three-dimensional realities.

Back at BP Mocamp we had our last dinner in the camp restaurant.

We ordered a loaf of bread "to go" in the morning. We told our little waiter Nechate that we were leaving and he was very sad.

August 1st:

Were ready to go at 8:00 and Nechate came down from the restaurant to deliver our loaf of bread and wish us a tearful goodbye.

Odom: at departure 8719

Chapter 14 ~ Bulgaria, Romania & Hungary

The border crossing into Bulgaria was tedious but the people we met appeared to be quite friendly. But then, we have found people friendly everywhere we went. It's just the little autocrats that leave the bad impression.

On the way to our camp in Kharmanli, Hugh and I stopped in a village to shop for eggs. When we walked into the little store, the other customers, mostly elderly women, just stared at us. It had never dawned on me that, perhaps, women in Bulgaria were not accustomed to seeing a strange woman in shorts walk into their store. We looked around and didn't see any eggs so I took a piece of paper out of my pocket, borrowed the clerk's pencil, and drew a very rough sketch of a chicken. They recognized it for what it was and when I drew eggs under the chicken they caught on. We got quite a few grins from the crowd, but no eggs. They pointed "away " and wrote down the number of kilometers to a larger community, there we would be able to get eggs. We thanked them profusely and headed out the door. We were walking back to the van when we spotted an ice cream vendor. She had a cart like hot dog vendors in Manhattan. She was selling soft ice cream and, of course, we each had to have a cone. It was good and not overpriced but the vendor took a fancy to the T-shirt I was wearing and wanted me to give it to her. She was quite insistent and I thought for a minute that she would yank it off but Hugh convinced her that it was my only shirt so she backed off.

We were looking forward to buying fresh eggs so were very happy to find the large grocery store the villagers had mentioned, but I couldn't find any eggs.

I still had my chicken and egg sketch so I approached a clerk and pointed out the eggs in the sketch. She was a formidable woman, and quite humorless. She glowered at me and pointed to the back of the store. But at the back of the store was the meat department. I showed the chicken and egg sketch to a butcher and he pointed to the shelf in front of the meat case and there, lo and behold, were paper bags containing six eggs. Who would have thought to look for eggs in paper bags? We carried our delicate burden to the check-out and were fortunate to get them safely stored in our little refrigerator.

After all that excitement we headed for Camping Gergana arriving at 4:30.

In Bulgaria we were obliged to eat at the camp restaurant. The meal (no choice) was pork chops.

There was a "duty free" shop across the street from the campground and we were able to buy Cadbury chocolate and top of the line scotch at a very low price, but the village stores had nothing. There were more bare shelves than stocked ones. The duty Free shop accepted Visa cards and collected their payments in American dollars.

Members of the Bulgarian football team, a boisterous, friendly group of young men, had rented a cottage next to out campsite. They befriended us in the morning and were interested in our journey. They offered us the use of their shower and bath but we were heading out so we didn't have the opportunity to accept their offer.

Miles today: 181 Odom: 8900

August 2nd:

On the road again at 8:15.(Willie Nelson where were you?) The scenery was a mix of pastoral and mountainous country and the traveling was easy. We used our gas coupons and after 202 miles, arrived at Camping Ribarska Koliba outside of Ruse.

Much to the chagrin of our "we got here first" couple, we had to wait until our leader arrived before we were admitted into the camp. The early birds waited for two fuming hours. I was tempted to remind them that it was a Slo'-Poke caravan®, but I refrained.

We had been forewarned in our log "some sites are not too level, facilities not too good or clean, bath tomorrow". That about describes it. We parked on the soccer field. It was the only level spot we found.

Miles today: 202 Odom: 9102

August 3rd:

Without regret we left Ruse at 8:30 a.m. Next stop, Romania.

From Bulgaria to Romania we crossed a bridge. Halfway across we were stopped by a soldier. He looked hot and weary and when Hugh rolled down his window to see what was required of us, the soldier peered in and said "You have coca cola?" Obviously he was thirsty and we did not have coca cola but we did have some lemonade. I poured him a paper cupful and he drained it. With a big smile, he waived us the rest of the way across the bridge into Romania.

We all lined up at the border and the customs people began at the front of our line going through every vehicle in turn. Somehow, as they approached us, they were distracted. The stepped off to the side and had a discussion. When their little debate was over, they returned to the string of Slo'-Poke® vans to continue their inspection. Evidently they had lost track of where they had stopped because they passed us by.

In Romania we had a guide assigned to us and we traveled in convoy. Things were much more communistic; every village had large red political billboards.

Here we were made far more aware of what life under communist rule was like. In camp we had an armed guard for our group. Romania had a jail overcrowding and released 6000 felons a few months before. As a result the crime rate was way up. An attempt to break in was made on one of our vans; the day before a tent in the park was sliced open.

A group of East German students were tent-camping close to us and I struck up a conversation with them. They were very hesitant at first but I guess they finally decided that my interest was genuine and that I had no ulterior motive.

They bemoaned the fact that they were only allowed to travel in the East; they would have loved to be able to go to Western Europe. They were certainly not happy with the communist regime in East Germany. In fact, they hinted that outright rebellion was a strong possibility.

In the evening we attended a Folklorico and had dinner across the street from the theater. I was very tired and did not feel well so I was happy to crawl into bed.

Miles today: 62 Odom: 9164

August 4th:

Another day spent in Bucharest. A city tour and shopping was on the agenda but I had a nasty stomach bug and stayed put. Hugh joined the Peters.

August 5th:

Next destination was Kluj-Turda over 250 miles ahead. Although I was feeling a little better I was beginning to long for our western world. We stopped in Cluj-Napoca and bought some lovely needlework made by the women. These people had not had coffee for two years. I had a pound of coffee beans in the cupboard that I had bought in Germany, never realizing that it was not ground coffee. Not having a grinder I had been unable to brew the coffee. I gave one of the ladies in the village the coffee figuring that she could probably break it up enough with a hammer to actually make a pot of coffee. She had tears in her eyes when I gave it to her. Later I was worried that I might have put her in jeopardy. Certainly someone would have smelled coffee brewing; would she have been reported and perhaps punished?

The one point of interest we visited was Count Dracula's castle. I was not impressed. We finally arrived at camp at 6:30. Dinner was included and all my log says about that is "Food Poor!." Our log also mentioned that, "sometimes the showers are warm." I can't remember if this was the camp where the showers were outside behind the building that housed toilets. I got pretty good at drawing the curtains in the van and taking a sponge bath standing in a basin.

Miles today: 300 Odom: 9464

August 6th:

Budapest.

By now both Hugh and I were suffering from great discomfort. If we had been in Mexico we have referred to our problem as having the "touristas." I had developed a maddening itchy rash to go along with the other problems. My log keeping suffered and I had to resort to "catch-up."

We had observed enough of life behind the iron curtain to know it was not a life we would chose. We did get a tour of Budapest, which is really a beautiful city. St. Stephen's Basilica is huge and is built on an imposing spot overlooking all of Budapest. The parking area was crowded with tour buses, some of which had brought in a large group of Russian soldiers. The natural reaction was to think of them as "the enemy." However, Hugh had been a soldier and his reaction was, " A soldier is a soldier; he does not make laws or rules. A soldier does what he is ordered to do by the powers that be." He chose to seek out a Russian non-commissioned officer and shake his hand as an act of friendship. I think the Russians were a little startled but in the end, they too were smiling.

Caravan '88

Photo #20 ~ Hugh & Russian Soldiers

There was one unpleasant incident at the cathedral; one of the Slo'-Pokers® lost his travelers checks when someone slit open the bottom of his backpack. His travelers checks were from Barclays bank and he was still waiting for replacements long after we left Budapest.

The campground in Budapest was mobbed. There were races scheduled in the area and fortunately we had been allotted a fenced in area just for our vans.

There were hot showers available but the whole camp was such a mess that I again resorted to drawn curtains and a sponge bath.

At this point I think we moved in a semi-coma condition; we couldn't wait to cross over into the free world.

Mileage: 270 Odom: 9724

Finally, on August 8th we entered Austria.

Chapter 15 ~ Austria and Lichtenstein

August 8th:

Finally we were back in the free world. The difference was incredible. Everything was clean, there were flowers everywhere, even the air felt different.

Our camp was in Laxenburg, just outside of Vienna and we had a bus tour of the city. Hugh skipped it because he still did not feel well but I wouldn't have missed Vienna for any reason. There is something about Vienna that makes you want to go back again and again. The whole atmosphere from Lippizan stallions to Johann Strauss to luscious pastry is the stuff of which great memories are made. I was fortunate enough to go back in 2000 and 2008.

August 10th:

We spent two wonderful recuperative days and then headed out to Melk. By now, although I hadn't kept my log up our odometer was 9919.

En route to Melk we stopped for propane and found a delightful spot for lunch in Weissenkirchen and arrived at the campground along the Danube river at 12:30 p.m.. We walked into town and shopped for a few things including ice cream, fresh pork and, of course, torte.

A lady in the camp at Melk took me to her doctor and he prescribed an antihistamine for the rash that had been tormenting me for days. I looked forward to not itching.
Tomorrow we leave for Berchtesgaden.

Miles today: 90 Odom: 10009

August 11th:

At 8 a.m. we left the camp at Melk, stopped in town to cash travelers checks and fill the gas tank. We avoided the Autobahn and traveled primarily on Rt #1 through picturesque countryside. We stopped for lunch on the shores of the Traunsee. The scenery was beautiful and the atmosphere was tranquil. Everything was so clean, it was a blessing to be out from behind the iron curtain.

Arrived at Berchtesgaden at 3:15 p.m. after 172 beautiful miles.

Odom: 10181

August 12th & 13th:

Beautiful countryside and lots to do with several treats from the "kitty" beginning with a boat trip on the Konigsee (Kings sea). This beautiful lake, nestled in the valleys between mountains, is the stuff of dreams and inspirations. I'm sure that more than one musical tribute has been written about it and that many more than one artists easel has been set up along it's banks.

Hugh and I did some meandering and shopping and I stopped at an apothecary to get more antihistamine. The pharmacist told me that the prescription I had received in Melk was really too strong and usually was prescribed for Asthmatic allergies. He recommended instead high doses of calcium and a cortisone cream. As a result, the itchy rash toned down a bit but the temperature did not. I had hoped that it would all go back to Bulgaria.

August 15th:

We left the beautiful Konigsee behind and headed for Garmiscch~Partenkirchen. This was some of the most beautiful scenery in the world, the Tyrolean Alps. I just wish I could have felt better; the fever wouldn't leave me. After arriving in Garmisch~Pattenkirchen I never even made a log entry other than to note that we made a side trip to Neu Schwanstein castle. It is the fairytale castle that was copied by Disney World for the Cinderella castle. (In 1994, when I was feeling a lot better, I finally had a tour of the whole castle.)

We evidently did some roaming from the time we arrived at Berchtesgaden, Our odometer on the morning of the 15th was 10545.

August 16th:

Our next destination—Vaduz in the tiny principality of Lichtenstein. All I could think of was finding a doctor. After a 111mile trip we pulled into the campground at Vaduz at 11 a.m. When we checked in I inquired at the desk where I could find a physician. The lady told us to go directly to the hospital and they would take care of me. We didn't even establish our campsite but headed right out to the hospital. I was amazed, there was no waiting line, no triage, I saw a doctor at once. He ordered a complete blood work up and we were asked to come back after lunch for the results. I asked if they could give me an estimate on the costs so that we could go to the bank and get Swiss francs. I was stunned when we were told there was no need to do that, they would just bill us later. After the initial shock (no one walks out of a hospital in the USA to be "billed later.") I explained that we would not be home until October and was told that was fine, they would bill us in October. (YES Virgina there is a Santa Claus!).

We wandered off and had some lunch and when we returned I saw the same doctor and he assured me that I was not dealing with allergies but that I had a viral infection. He gave me a prescription for vitamin C (1000mg) and fever suppositories. The C Vitamins looked like the old Necco Wafers we used to buy in the candy store, the size of a silver dollar. At that point I would even have settled for the Necco wafers.

When we returned to the campground I thanked the personnel for directing us to the hospital. As soon as we were parked in our assigned space, I curled up and slept until suppertime. Hugh was not feeling any better. We just rested the next day before heading into Switzerland.

The hospital was true to its' word, a bill arrived in Florida in mid-October addressed, not to Hugh McCafferty or Ursula McCafferty but to HughUrsula (no last name). It's a good thing that we were well known in our park.

Miles: 119 Odom: 10664

Chapter 16 ~ Switzerland

August 18th:

At 8:30 a.m. the Swiss Alps loomed ahead of us. The grandeur of mountains and the villages nestled in the tight valleys were picture perfect.

Driving in the Alps is like riding a roller-coaster all day… breathtaking.

We stopped several times to just take in the beauty and we gave a couple of hikers a lift on a long uphill. We both were still battling a low fever and looked forward to an early supper and an early-to-bed. We arrived at the camp in Visp in the early afternoon, weary and still under the weather.

Miles today: 146 Odom: 10810

Photo #20 ~ Typically Swiss

August 19th:

A "kitty treat" was on the schedule today, a trip on the cog railway to Zermatt. Again, Hugh and I skipped it because we were just too tired. However, I really wanted to see the Matterhorn so we took off on our own.

We had lunch in Zermatt and got some great pictures of the Matterhorn. Fortunately the air was clear and the mountain was in full view. Of course we did not shop in Zermatt. Prices in Switzerland were higher than in Lichtenstein and I had thought that they were high there.

Miles today: 36 Odom: 10846

August 20th:

A short days trip took us Villenevue. It rained all the way and the weather was chilly. It would have been a great day to curl up in a recliner in front of a cozy fire with a good book (and a box of chocolates!)

We had dinner in the park restaurant and it was superb and very expensive.

Miles today: 72 Odom: 10918

August 21st:

A free day with lots of choices. Groups teamed up going hither and   yon…lunch at Mt. Blanc with a ride through the longest tunnel in the world, a visit to Challon Castle just 2.3 miles from camp. Hugh and I were still a bit under the weather so we took a day off the road. We did do the laundry but other than that we just took a walk, a nap and dinner out. It was an enjoyable and relaxing day.

August 22nd:

We left Villeneuve at 7:30 for Interlaaken where Hugh and I would take a few days off to visit friends and relatives in Germany. We planned to rejoin the caravan at Rothenburg ob der Tauber. The trip to Interlaaken was an easy run through picturesque country. We arrived at the park at 11 a.m. just as it began to rain. We decided to head out on our solo journey right away. We spent all our Swiss francs in Basel, rolled into Germany and pulled into a rest area on the Autobahn for the night.

Chapter 17 ~ Back to Germany

August 23rd:

We slept pretty well, despite vehicles coming and going through the rest areas during he night. As soon as we felt we weren't getting anyone out of bed, we called my nephew. He gave us directions to his home and we made plans to see them in the early evening.. We left the Autobahn and traveled on highway #3 with no log instructions, just a good road map. Mid morning we reached the town of Kenzingen and took a break. Hugh found a barber and got a haircut; we had lunch in a tavern and the food was great. After lunch we took a leisurely walk and visited the church. Then I had a treat; I had my first perm since Andorra. It was such a relaxing, satisfying day and we both seemed to have finally shaken the "bug form Bulgaria."

We arrived at my nephew's house at six and spent a lovely evening with him and his wife. When it was time to leave he gave us directions to a great campsite not far from his home. The facilities were immaculate and I decided to have a nice hot shower before bedtime. There was only one snag…the lights in the building were on some sort of timer and when I was barley out of the shower the building lights went out. Fortunately, from habit, I had a flashlight with me. I wrapped myself in a towel, went to the door of the building, opened the door and the lights went on again. I didn't even take the time to dry my hair, I just dressed and escaped before the lights went out again.

I telephoned my two cousins, Erica and Olga (nicknamed Dix), and made plans to visit Erica the next day.

Miles since Interlaaken: 388 Odom: 11306.

August 24th:

With instructions to Erica's home we headed out in the morning. We stopped to fill our propane tank and have lunch in, of all places, a real Pizza Hut.

We found Erica's home in Trippstadt and spent a lovely few hours visiting the cousin I had never met. Erica was the daughter of my father's only sister. It was quite a thrill to meet "family." We stayed two hours and then set out to continue our journey. I never saw Erica again. She passed away about a year after our visit.

After leaving Trippstadt we began a southeasterly track. It was Wednesday afternoon and we were going to visit cousin Dix on Friday. We found a good rest area between Offenburg and Freiburg, and called daughter Penny to let the family know we were presently Off Caravan.

Miles today: 161 Odom: 11467

August 25th:

We spent the whole day just roaming through the Black Forest. Seeing the density of the evergreen forest, it was easy to see why it had been named the Black Forest. The air was filled with the scent of pine and balsam and the whole area had a fairy tale quality about it. We stopped in a small village and ate lunch and then continued our roaming until early evening. The weather had turned showery. At 6 p.m. we found a lovely campground near Freudenstadt and checked in for the night. As in most German campgrounds, we were able to order rolls for breakfast.

Mileage today: 101 miles Odom: 11568

August 26th:

We were really lazy; we slept late and then picked up our fresh, warm rolls and dawdled over breakfast and then did laundry. The camp had a good washer and dryer and even an ironing board and iron so I was able to iron my suit. We finally left the camp right after lunch and headed for Stuttgart to visit cousin Dix. We found the senior assisted living apartment where she lived and were quite impressed how nice the complex was. I hadn't seen Dix since she was four and I was five. I don't think either one of us would have remembered the other had we passed each other on a street. Even though Hugh spoke no German and Dix spoke no English, they got along amazingly well. Dix wanted us to stay for supper but we were anxious to leave in daylight so we could find a camp for the night so we said our goodbye at 5:30. We stopped in a highway rest area and had supper. It had begun to rain so we were fortunate to spot a camping sign at 6:30. The camp was called Hirtenteich, which translates to "shepherd's pond".

Miles today: 100 Odom: 11668

August 27th:

It was time to rejoin the caravan at Rothenburg ob der Tauber. We left Hirtenteich at 10 a.m. and had a rainy drive to join our group. We arrived at Camping Tauber-Idyll on the "Romantische Strasse " (romantic road) in Rothenburg at 4:30 p.m. The campground was just down the hill from the historic walled town of Rothenburg that we planned to visit the following day.

Mileage today: 101 Odom: 11769

August 28th:

The campground was located on a picturesque country road where Hugh took a stroll in the morning. He had picked up a few German words by then and he put them to great use. He passed a lovely garden and stopped to admire it. The owner was out weeding and she turned to see who was at her fence. Hugh greeted her and, with a mixture of German and charades, explained to the lady that her flowers were lovely and that his wife loved flowers. Whether she took pity on his attempt to speak German or his ham acting I'll never know. I do know that he returned to camp with a huge bouquet of flowers for me. I thought, "Good grief, he's raided someone's garden" but when he told me what he had said and done, I gave him a triple A for effort. His German went something like this, "Schoene

Blumen,(lovely flowers), meine Frau (my wife) "AAAH Blumen!" ending by a hand over the heart and a big sigh! What a HAM. God bless him.

We took the bus up to Rothenburg rather than walk the long steep road. The town is a delight albeit touristy. It is completely walled in and dates back 900 years. During the Thirty Years War the town, which was Protestant, was captured by the Catholic troops. The commander of the Catholic troops had planned to torch the town but he gave the councilman an opportunity to save the town. If the councilman could drink a liter of ale in one long draft without stopping the town would be spared. The councilman succeeded and to honor that great accomplishment there is a clock in the town hall to celebrate the event. On the hour a door opens and a figure representing the councilman rolls out and lifts a large stein going through the motions of chug-a-lugging a liter of ale. There is always a crowd on hand in the square to watch this re-enactment of the heroic councilman's deed.

We took the stairs to the top of the town wall and walked around the perimeter.

Looking down on this medieval town gave us a wonderful overview. I fell in love with the place and managed to return to it on several occasions in later years. Rothenburg is the idyllic town where the movie of Hansel and Gretel was filmed.

August 29th:

Time to move on to Neckergemund. This should have been an easy run but it turned into confusion. When we reached the town of Mockmuhl certain roads were blocked off because of construction. We thought we were turning at the right places and in the right direction. However, when we, for the third time, arrived at the riverbank and saw the same barge tied up at the same dock, we knew we had gone wrong somewhere. There were signs which we had really not understood until I finally let the legend on the sign sink in. The sign said, "UMLEITUNG." "Um" means around, "leitung" means leading together they mean DETOUR! We knew that we were on the wrong side of the river but decided to just follow Routet #37 and the Neckar river until we saw signs for Neckergemund; there would have to be a bridge somewhere.

The trip downriver was very enjoyable. It was a scenic drive and there was much activity on the river. We stopped for lunch at a lovely restaurant right on the water. Before too long we spotted our first sign for our destination. There was a sturdy bridge to cross and we could see some of our caravan already parked at rivers edge across the bridge.

Photo #21 ~ Camp at Neckergemund

There was a great celebration in progress in Neckergemund, the town was celebrating its' 1000 birthday. We camped right on the shore and adjoining the campground was a huge tent where all the town festivities were taking place. Beer was being tapped into the tent directly from large beer tankers. A fashion show and dancing were scheduled for the evening and food was available.

We spent part of the afternoon feeding swans and ducks that came right up to the bank looking for a handout. The traffic on the river was fun to watch, so many different types of vessels cruising by.

I could have spent a week in that spot. In fact, Hugh and I returned to that campsite in 1992.

Supper in the tent was great and tables were available for as many Slo'-Pokers® as wanted to partake. I would have loved to stay for the dancing but the fashion show was still going strong at ten and I was too tired to stay up and don't drink beer so I hit the sack. Hugh stayed with it a little longer.

Miles today: 105 Odom: 11874

August 30th:

We took the ferry downstream to Heidelburg; the ferry passes through two locks on the way. Heidleburg is the wonderful place featured in the operetta *The Student Prince*. The main street is a pedestrian way with shops, restaurants and open-air markets. The university is a wonderful old world structure for learning. The restaurant *Zum Roten Ochs* (To the Red Ox) is a student favorite. Of course they feature the music of the operetta: Deep in My Heart, The Drinking Song and more.

The old towered bridge that crosses the Neckar is a national landmark.

Heidelburg is a delightful place to spend a day. I hated to leave. We returned to camp via bus rather than try to meet a ferry schedule. We spent the rest of the afternoon just loafing and watching the river traffic; it was very relaxing. Tomorrow we're on the road again, this time to Bingen on the Rhine river.

August 31st:

An easy run to Bingen. We didn't stop en route for lunch, just had a sandwich on arrival at 1 p.m. The camp was located about 100 yards from the remains of a bombed out railroad bridge the "Hindenburg Bridge." The bridge was destroyed in WWII and never rebuilt.

We found a good supermarket in the village and stocked our larder. In the evening we took the ferry across the Rhine to the quaint town of Rudesheim.

We had a nice dinner, a pleasant stroll and an early return to camp. The Rhine Cruise was scheduled for the following day.

September 1st:

No Rhine cruise is complete without all three stanzas of the "Lorelei" being played on the PA system. As we went "sailing down the river" past the "Maus Torm" (Mouse Tower) and the fabled "Lorelei" I sang, quite unashamedly, right along with the music. (I know all three verses in German!).

The weather was ideal for a morning cruise and we all came back energized; singing will do that to you.

September 2nd:

The next day Hugh and I took off to explore. We took a road in Bachrach leading away from the river and over a mountain. We wound up at a beautiful overlook, equipped with a picnic table. I made coffee and sandwiches for our lunch. We sat at the picnic table to eat and just watch the Rhine flow by below us, pure pleasure!

Meandered 50 miles today: Odom: 12030

September 3rd:

On to Köln (Cologne)! The journey took us via Koblenz and Bonn on Route #42. In Bonn we picked up the autobahn and then the fun began. We overshot our exit by several miles and had to find our way back. Fortunately we made it to camp by noon with no further mix-up. Managed to visit the twin-spired cathedral which was the model for St. Patrick's Cathedral in New York City.

Our time on this great journey is fast drawing to an end. Hard to believe that we left home in April.

Miles today: 110 Odom: 12140

Chapter 18 ~ On to Great Britain

September 4th:

At 9:a.m., it was time to leave my native land again. Belgium is next.

The trip to Gent was on the super highway A40 all the way and uneventful.

The campground was neat, clean and well appointed with laundry, store, bar and restaurant. We are all getting keyed up for the British Isles tomorrow.

Miles today: 181 Odom: 12321

September 5th:

We rolled out of camp around 8 a.m. and made the 39 miles to the dock at Ostende by 9a.m. All but three of us managed to get on the 10 a.m. ferry.

After a gray crossing we landed in Dover in the sunshine. It was amazing to finally see the White Cliffs of Dover. When we drove off the ferry an attendant waved at each of us and yelled "Drive LEFT!" It was at that moment that Hugh thought I should have some driving experience. Fortunately I overcame the urge to drive right in a hurry.

We arrived at Abbey Woods campsite at 4 p.m. Hot showers and hot water for dishes were available but no clothes lines were permitted so there was not much point in doing a load of laundry. We decided to wait until we could find a laundry. Tomorrow there is a scheduled bus tour of London and then Hugh and I will separate, temporarily, from the Caravan again. We plan to visit our son-in-law's family in Bognor Regis and then head up into Scotland so Hugh can visit Ayr, find his old home and have a walk down memory lane.

Miles today: 112 Odom: 12433

September 6th:

The bus tour around London was great. There was so much to see from Big Ben to the Palace, the Tower of London, Crown jewels, London Bridge—almost more than one could absorb in one half day. Our tour was supposed to return us back to Abbey Woods camp by 2:45 p.m. but it became evident that that was not going to happen. We had an appointment with our son-in-law James' family for 6 p.m. in Bognor Regis so our caravan leader, Jim, gave us train fare back to camp and had the bus driver drop us at a train station. We packed up and rolled out, made one stop to cash Travelers checks and buy a hostess gift for James' mother. I had been to the house in Bognor a few years earlier so we had no trouble locating it. The house is a landmark, designed and built by James great-uncle. It's called The White Tower and was the tallest building in Bognar when it was built. Since then an apartment house was built directly across the street cutting off a view of the Channel.

We actually arrived in time for dinner. James' sister and her husband were there to greet us as well. It was a nice opportunity for Hugh to meet the family and it was a pleasure to spend the night in real beds again.

Miles today: 74 Odom: 12507

September 7th:

Today we were introduced to Sainsburys, the English supermarket. James' mother Kathleen joined us. We bought lots of "stock-up" food and then drove on to the lovely little village of Charlton to visit James' sister. The village is a delight; many of the cottages have thatched roofs and everyone has a garden.

James' uncle Martin had lived in a thatched cottage in Charlton. I had a tour of that one when Martin was still alive. It had been built in the 1400s and was obviously built for people shorter than Martin's six-foot frame. I can remember him stooping to go through doorways between the upper rooms of the cottage. It was lovely and looked like something one would expect to find on a calendar or in a book about Shakespeare.

We returned to Bognor in early afternoon, had an early dinner and after dinner Hugh and I took a walk along the beach. We spent another night sleeping in real beds. We planned to continue our journey in the morning.

Miles in Bognor area: 40 Odom: 12547

September 8th:

Left Bognar right after a typical English breakfast of bacon, eggs, fried tomato and toast and headed north. We just meandered along. We saw signs for Stone Henge and decided it was something we really wanted to see. The place is amazing…how could a primitive people ever have created such an extraordinary "temple." I call it a temple for want of a better description.

From Stone Henge we headed up to Cirencester, the town where our daughter Penny had gone to Equestrian school and where she met her husband James who was a fellow student. We located Talland Equestrian Center and enjoyed seeing the place where our daughter received her British Horse Society certification. After a very relaxed, enjoyable day, we tapped into some of our supplies from Sainsburys and had a nice dinner before bedding down for the night.

Mileage today: 135 Odom: 12682

September 9th:

The showers were hot, breakfast was good and we were ready to go by 9:30. Today we used the M5 motorway to move us northward a little faster.

We made several rest stops along the M5 and found a campground in the Lake District at the foot of Lake Windermere at 4:45. The northwest county of Cumbria is very picturesque with lakes nestled among the hills and winding country roads.

We called son Pat and asked him to arrange a family reunion dinner at a local restaurant for our homecoming. Also called Penny and told her about our visit Talland. It was a long day just driving; it was an "early to bed" night. Tomorrow we must find a Laundromat!

Miles today: 248 Odom: 12930

September 19th:

We got a good start at 8:30. It was cloudy and the narrow roads made for slow travel but the scenery was spectacular. We had hoped to find a laundry in Penrith but couldn't find a place to park. We decided to get back to motorway travel and headed for the M6. The traffic was heavy but we rolled right along and drove right to Ayr. Found a great spot "Heads of Ayr Caravan Park" a bit south of the town. As soon as we were checked in we made good use of the laundry facility.

The location of the Caravan Park brought back so many memories for Hugh. The office and Pub were actually situated on the spot that had been the railroad platform when Hugh was living in Ayr. The "Heads of Ayr" are cliffs and below the cliffs are areas of sandy beach (and very cold water.) Hugh's family used to take the excursion train from town out to the Heads, follow the trail down to the beach and picnic. I put one toe into the frigid water and wondered if they all turned blue when they swam there?

We chatted with a gentleman who was a regular member of the park. He told us that he owned the Victoria Pub in town. Hugh couldn't believe it. The Victoria Pub had been Hugh's father's pub before his family moved to the USA.

It is, indeed, a small world.

Arrived at 3:30 p.m. Miles: 167 Odom: 13097

September 11th:

Today we explored Ayr. We found Hugh's last home in Scotland at Beresford Terrace, lunched in Dunure, visited the Robert Burns

Center, the "Old Brig", found a great super market and spent a second night at Heads of Ayr in heavy rain and wind.

Miles exploring today: 40 Odom: 13137

September 12th:

We were back on the road by 8:30, bought propane and got cash from the automatic teller at the bank. We had to make tracks to meet the caravan at Maidenhead in time for our ferry crossing to Ireland.

We made a stop in Dunfries looking for a special souvenir for our son-in law; James has a collection of small gauge model trains and we wanted to buy an item to add to his collection. We were not able to find anything so we continued as far as Ings, back in the Lake country, and camped for the night.

Miles today: 196 Odom: 13333

September 13th:

After a leisurely breakfast, we pointed our van southwestward through the beautiful Snowdonia National Park in North Wales and onward to Holyhead.

We arrived at the ferry to Ireland terminal at 6:00 p.m. and rejoined our group.

It was great to see all our fellow travelers again and to swap tales of adventures with them.

Miles today: 252 Odom: 13585

September 14th:

The realization, that our time on this journey is growing short, is sinking in. By this time next month we all be home again in the good old USA.

It was a short night. We were awake at 1:30 a.m., up at 3:30 and boarding the ferry at 4:30. The ferry trip took 3 ½ hours and landed us in Dublin. We were tired and hungry and still had miles to go. We did take a break for breakfast and then rolled along to Powers the Pot Camp in Clonmel.

Arrived at 3:30 p.m. after total mileage today: 151 Odom: 13736

The Camp had hot showers and a quaint barroom with a turf fireplace but all that registered with us was the cold wind and a sense of desolation. We were very tired and had no desire to spend our evening in the bar so it was an "early to bed" night and we planned to depart on our own again in the morning.

September 15th:

On our own again. We left Clonmel camp at 9 a.m. and wandered down through Cork to the coast. Highway N71 led us down to Skibberreen where we found a Tourist information center. Fortunately they had a good book with campground information and we were able to find a really great campground right on the shore of Bantry Bay, Eagle Point Camping and Caravan Park. The park was beautiful and immaculate, equipped with 2 washing machines and two dryers, always a plus when you're traveling. The fee was 6 Irish pounds and very well worth it.

Arrived at 5 p.m. Miles today: 160 Odom: 13896

September 16th:

Used the laundry facilities before leaving Eagle Point. It's always a blessing when we can start the day without a bag of laundry waiting to be washed. It was about noon when we finally hit the road to Killarney to join the group. We just poked along stopping for breaks and photos. We had no problems finding Beech Grove campground. We arrived at 4 p.m. after a short run, 57 miles. The campground had possibilities but would have been much nicer with a little better housekeeping. It couldn't hold a candle to Eagle Point.

Odom: 13953

September 17th:

Spent the day on a great bus tour of the "Ring of Kerry". There were sheep everywhere—in the road and in the fields. Many of them had bright colored patches on the backs and we joked about the pre-dyed wool. Actually the dye patches had something to do with which ewes were bred but pre-dyed wool was a less complicated description.

We were amazed at whole hedges of fuchsias in full bloom along the roadside.

I had no idea that they grew into shrubs having only seen them as potted plants.

We had the opportunity to do some souvenir shopping but we didn't see much sunshine.

In the morning we're going solo again, reconnecting with group in Dublin.

September 18th:

Left camp at 8 a.m. and followed the coast road around the south side of Galway Bay. Another cloudy day! At lunch time we pulled off the road on a small strip of beach, ate a leisurely lunch and wandered around a bit before moving on.

At 3:30 we found a lovely campground at Hodson Bay near Athalone, County Roscommon. There were no washing machines available but we did wash our duffle bags and Hugh's carryon. They had begun to smell a bit musty from having been stored up top. After chores we had dinner and a short walk around the park before calling it a night. Tomorrow we'll have a 70 mile run to Dublin; the next day back to Scotland.

Miles today: 200 Odom: 14153

September 19th:

Another Willie Nelson "On the road again" at 10:30. There was no need for haste today. The run to Dublin was less than one hundred miles. We spent the last of our Irish pounds for a Pub lunch, candy and enough for the toll bridge over the river Liffey.

The facilities at Cromlech Caravan Park included the "always welcome" hot showers, a small store and level parking.

Miles today: 96 Odom: 14249

September 20th:

To make our connection with the ferry to Scotland, we left camp at 7:30 a.m. We soaked up as much of the Irish landscape, mist and rainbows for our memory banks as we could.

The border crossing into Northern Ireland was a unique experience for us.

The armed border guard was intrigued. Several of our vans had already crossed the border when we arrived. We were stopped and our first reaction was "OOOPS, what have we done?" Fortunately we hadn't "done" anything; the guard was just curious. He leaned on the open window and prepared to chat about all the Volkswagons...what group were we, where were we going, where had we been etc... all this while border traffic was backing up behind us. We thoroughly enjoyed the chat, not so the backed up traffic. In spite of our lengthy chat at the border crossing we arrived at ferry terminal in Larne early enough for lunch.

At 3:30 we boarded the ferry for Stranraer, Scotland. The crossing was uneventful and we docked at 5:50. Once we all disembarked we made the short run to the Cairnryan Caravan and Chalet Park. We took one look at the crowded conditions and split for Ayr, arriving at Heads of Ayr Park at 7:30 p.m.. Had a great dinner in the pub and visited with the other guests of the park.

Total miles today: 191 Odom: 14440

September 21st:

Spent a leisurely day driving around town, shopping and sight-seeing. Hugh was on a long walk down Memory Lane. In the past he always said he didn't want to go back to Scotland because you can't "go back" but he really did enjoy his time in Ayr and surroundings.

September 22nd:

Just 2 more weeks of wandering before the journey home. We bid farewell to the Heads of Ayr and David Semple, the owner of the park at 10 a.m. Stopped for a last look at Ayr and filled our propane in Prestwick. It was a day to wander through cloudy weather towards Balloch. We crossed the mountains to Long Loch and Gareloch. From there we followed the north shore and cut across at Tarbet, then along the south shore of Loch Lomond, arriving at the campground in Balloch at 4:00 p.m.

It began to rain shortly after our arrival but it was a nice clean park.

Miles today: 119 Odom: 14578

September 23rd:

After a night of steady rain, our route today took us from Balloch to Inverness. The steady rain had let up but all day there were showers interspersed with beautiful rainbows. We drove passed Loch Ness but saw no sign of Nessie, the fabled Loch Ness monster. In Ft. William we took a lunch break and did some shopping. Rolled into camp at 4:15.

Miles today: 153 Odom: 14731

September 24th:

Today was a free day and we went exploring. We went into town but there was no place to park in the center of Inverness; but we did get to *James Pringle Weavers* wonderful shop. The clothing was absolutely beautiful. The tartans were available for any clan in Scotland. There were kilts, warm sweaters and shawls for any occasion. I could have blown a small fortune (if I had one).

However, no longer living in the northeast but in sunny Florida, I would hardly have had use for them. We did buy woven wool and mohair shawls for some of our daughters-in-law. From Pringles we took a drive to Dingwell and Tain and crossed back to Inverness via

Beauly. We saw lots of offshore oil rigs, drove through showers off and on and saw lots of rainbows. We finally got back to camp at 4:15. It was a great day and was topped off by a super fireworks display in the evening.

Miles today: 120 Odom: 14851

September 25th:

This morning we slept in a bit and then began the trek to Edinburgh via Aberdeen. Our instructions took us on the M90 to a junction with the M9. We never found the M9 and, as a result, we couldn't follow the rest of the log directions. The express highways are no place to stop and ask directions so we got horribly lost. We were finally able to pull off the highway and find help.

Once we got turned back to the right directions we arrived safely at camp at 4 p.m. After all the confusion and frustration the day ended with a great experience. We were treated to *"A Taste of Scotland."* Of all the great "kitty treats" we had, this was the best. The entire presentation, from dancing, bagpipes and piping in the Hagiss was traditional Scotland. It was wonderful; I think Hugh was in seventh heaven.

Miles today: 255 Odom: 15106

September 26th:

After a late night out we slept in again. Decided to skip the tour of Edinbugh. After being lost there yesterday we had no great desire to return.

Instead we did laundry and headed out to our next rendezvous. We were to meet in Peterborough on 9/27; that gave us a whole day to wander and do some last minute shopping in "bonnie Scotland."

September 26th:

We spent the morning doing chores and laundry and then headed out.

We had lots of time to wander today. We took pictures, stopped to eat, took a few side roads and loafed. It was nice and easy and no tight schedule. Found a good campground in Appleby-in-Westmoreland. After dinner and a nice stroll we called it a day.

Miles today: 138 Odom: 15244

September 27th:

Our route today took us to Carlisle so we took a chance, looked for a store that sold model trains. We got lucky; we found the model train and a few other goodies. I was hoping for a hair salon and we found one in a mall in Orton. When I entered the shop I had some misgivings based on the age and style of the clientele and the stylists. I figured nothing much could go wrong with a shampoo and haircut. I should have listened to the inner me. My hair was washed and clipped and styled in a jiffy. The "style" would have been really neat on a teeny-bopper. I didn't dare ask her to change anything for fear it would be worse. She was very pleased with the outcome and thought I would be delighted to be so much more "with-it".

When I rejoined Hugh he looked at me, shook his head and said, "You paid for that?" My only comfort was that I knew it would grow in or out or something before I got back home. I still had nine days!

We arrived Ferry Meadows Caravan Club in Peterborough at 2:45. The showers were hot and the park was only 1 mile from town, convenient for any last minute shopping.

Miles today: 204 Odom: 15448

Chapter 19~ Back to the Continent

September 28th:

We departed at 7:15 from our last camp in Great Britain and headed for the ferry to Belgium. The crossing was uneventful and we arrived at our camp in Brugge at 6:15.

Miles today: 134 Odom: 15582.

The tour was now scheduled to head eastward again with an opportunity to visit Berlin. I still had friends to see in Germany and I wanted to visit my home town, Hamburg. Neither one of us really wanted to cross over into the east zone again. We had seen enough of life on the other side of the Berlin wall.

We would return to Wiedenbruck and the VW plant on October 2nd. All the rigs would have to undergo some fuel conversions before they were shipped home. That gave us three more days on our own.

September 29th:

At 8:15 we left the camp at Brugge and started another journey into personal history. Our targets were Elsfleth, my mother's place of birth, and Hamburg, my home town. In Hamburg we planned to reconnect with Schoelgels, the couple we had met at our first camp in Tecklenburg way back in April.

It was nice to wander through small villages, stopping in small roadside rests for coffee breaks and lunch. The German countryside is quite picturesque so we took lots of photos to supplement the memories we would carry home with us.

At 5:30 we were watching for campground signs but hadn't seen any all afternoon. We stopped for supper in the village of Quackenbruck and did some souvenier shopping. We asked about any nearby camping facility and the clerk in the shop gave us directions to a quiet country road with ample parking where we could safely spend the night. We had done enough dry camps before so that wasn't a problem. It was a cool night but we had a good nights sleep with no interruption.

Miles today: 327 Odom: 15909

September 30th:

We got back on the road at 8 a.m. and took our time wandering up to Elsfleth. When we arrived in town we visited the cemetery to look for family names. We found my grandparents graves and the graves of the family that raised my mother after her mother died. We met a lady in the cemetery and I asked her about the house in which my mother had lived. She was so enthusiastic that she ran to several different homes looking for information.

With her help we found #10 Weser Strasse where my mom had grown up.

We also saw the site of the Merchant marine Academy where my father was trained for his life at sea. It was while he was at school in Elsfleth that he met my mother and where they had married 78 long years ago.

There was no camping facility in Elsfleth so we continued on our journey. En route to the Autobahn we spotted a camping sign in Delmenhorst. It was 4 p.m. and the days were getting shorter so, rather than drive after dark looking for a place, we pulled in for the night. There was a good restaurant on site so we had a leisurely dinner. After dinner we phoned Schoegels in Hamburg and arranged to meet them at the Stillhorn rest area on the Autobahn the next day.

Miles today: 212 Odom: 16121

October 1st:

Woke to a chilly morning 3 degrees Celsius, 37 Fahrenheit, Brrrrr.

At 9 a.m. we started the run to Hamburg. It was autobahn all the way but we did get screwed up. Somehow, we missed the Stillhorn rest area. There was no way to get across multi lanes of traffic so we had to get off the eastbound autobahn, get on the westbound, pass Stillhorn and reenter autobahn at the next eastbound ramp back to Stillhorn. When our friends arrived they led us back to their home where we parked our camper. Then we were taken on a great tour of the city of Hamburg.

Miles today: 110 Odom: 16231

I got to see the apartment where I had lived until I was 4 years old, (104 Koppel). I will never forget that address because when I was small it was drummed into me. Even though my speech was still childish I learned to say "I live at Koppel 104" in case I ever got lost.

We visited the Tietz Department store where I remember going with my mother. On cold winter days they had hostesses walking through the store serving hot beef broth. The "Konditorei" (pastry shop) was located on the top floor of the store and they used to sell huge creampuffs filled with whipped cream. All through the years I promised myself that if I ever got back to Hamburg I would go to Tietz and have coffee and a creampuff. Well, I had made it back. We headed up to the pastry shop and I was practically drooling.

When I didn't see any creampuffs in the showcase I asked if they had any and then heard the sad news, "It's Saturday, we don't make them on Saturday."

Sometimes fate can be cruel! Of course, with all the pastry already consumed on this odyssey in France, Germany and Austria, it was probably a blessing that Tietz did not bake creampuffs on Saturday.

There were some really highpoints for me on this visit to Hamburg. Not only did I see where I had lived, I actually got to see some of the fireworks display across the Alster River. I remember sitting on our 4th floor porch and watching firework displays across the Alster when I was four years old. I was delighted to find reference to those fireworks on Google. It's nice to know that some traditions continue.

After a full day of sightseeing we returned to Schoegel's home for dinner and planning for their visit to USA in 1989. They plan to rent our camper and spend six weeks touring our country. We finally had to call it a night. The following day would be a busy one, preparing for the journey home.

Current Odom reading: 16244

October 2nd:

After breakfast Schoegel's led us back to the Stillhorn rest area on the autobahn. We said our goodbye and at 11a.m. we headed for Wiedenbruck and the VW plant to have the necessary alterations made to our van before they were shipped home.

Arrived at Westfalia Works plant at 3:30 p.m. Beginning at approximately 7 a.m. each van will be driven into the shop in turn. We are not permitted in the plant but will be able to leave for Bremen as soon as our own van is returned to us. We will gather again at the campground in Bremen.

Miles today: 149 Odom: 16393

October 3rd:

Our vehicle was ready for us to head out at 3 p.m. It was autobahn to Bremen all the way. We made camp at 5:30, had an early supper and began sorting our equipment...what would be left in the van and what was going home with us. Knowing that the next day and night would be busy and rest would be scarce, we opted for an early to bed.

Miles today: 110 Odom: 16503

October 4th:

We took the time for a good breakfast and then set to work. We packed and repacked. We had bought a lovely brass lantern in Turkey; we wondered how best to pack it in one of our duffle bags. Then the light dawned...we had a pail! Wrapped in a blanket and stuffed with our laundry for cushion the lantern was neatly packed in the pail in one duffle bag! It made the trip home without a scratch. Since we would not be doing any laundry before leaving, the laundry, stuffed into plastic bags, made great cushions for anything breakable.

Camping gear would stay in the vehicle; we had purchased insurance to cover contents of the van.

I originally planned to contact a cousin while in Bremen but we just didn't have time to visit. Looking back it seems to have taken us all day to get organized but it is amazing how much "stuff" you can accumulate in a Volkswagon camper in 6 months. I think our group probably filled every trash barrel in the park.

At the end of the day we had left out clean clothes for the trip home, enough food for the following day, gotten rid of any perishables and packed anything worth saving. We were TIRED! The next day it would be onward to Emden and the pier where our vans would be loaded on a transport ship and we would be bussed to Amsterdam for the flight home.

October 5th:

We took our time leaving for Emden. It was only a 110-mile trip and once there, there would nothing to do but wait. We dawdled over breakfast, stopped for several coffee breaks and lunch and arrived at our appointed spot in plenty of time to fill out all the necessary paper work. We were parked on the pier and the huge container ship was right there. We were to be ready for the bus, luggage out and car locked at 4 a.m. Needless to say, we were all so keyed up that none of us got much sleep. We were going HOME! The great adventure was coming to an end.

Miles today: 110 Odom: 16613

And to think we started with 0 miles in April.

As promised, the bus arrived at 4 a.m.; surprisingly (or maybe not) everyone was ready to go. I think we all were ready to go HOME! It had been a really wonderful experience; we had seen so much of the world and so much of the different living conditions but now we could look forward to family reunions and our own safe, comfortable environment.

We loaded our trusty duffle bags on the bus and settled down for the trip to Schiphol airport and the homeward flight.

We had no problems with the flight back to O'Hare in Chicago but we still had miles to go. First on our agenda was to retrieve our car from the mushroom farm. We took a taxi to the farm and were led to our vehicle, deep in the bowels of the shed. We were handed our keys, loaded on our duffle bags and climbed in. I turned the ignition key and got NOTHING! The battery was deader than a doornail, why I will never know. So rather than heading for Connecticut to a family reunion, we were towed to a Chrysler dealership for a new battery.

Fortunately the job was accomplished in minimal time and we were on our way.

Putting this together has been a wonderful experience. I made the trip twice, once in fact and once down memory lane.

About the Author

Ursula McCafferty was born in Germany, and has been an American citizen since 1933. She is a retired US Postmaster, widow, mother of 5, grandmother of 12, and Great Grandmother of 4. This is her 3rd book about her 5½-month travel trip to Europe in 1988. Her second book is a biographical memoir about her father, and her first book is a story of her family growing up.

Made in the USA
Charleston, SC
09 November 2013